Life Lessons

Jan Shepherd

To: Bill Bagents
Christmas 2003
With thanks for your good work and
great helpfulness in our graduate
program.

— Coy Roper
Director of Graduate Studies

Life Lessons

◆

A roadmap to surviving life's twists and turns

Ian James Shepherd

iUniverse, Inc.
New York Lincoln Shanghai

Life Lessons
A roadmap to surviving life's twists and turns

iUniverse, Inc.

For information address:
iUniverse, Inc.
2021 Pine Lake Road, Suite 100
Lincoln, NE 68512
www.iuniverse.com

ISBN: 0-595-27880-9

Printed in the United States of America

For Dee Ann, Tabitha, Ethan, Mum, Dad, Steve, Sue and all those in our extended family who made me laugh out loud.

Contents

Foreword

When I acquired the author of these essays as a son-in-law, I knew our daughter was getting a good man, a Christian from a good family, who would support her and love her for all of their lives together. And I was right. He has proved to be a good husband, a good provider, a good son-in-law, and a great father.

What I didn't know—even though I've known him since he was twelve—was that he was a talented writer. (There were a few other things I didn't know, too—about what he did when he was five-years-old, for instance, but those things will become obvious in the book.) But when he started composing the essays found in this book and sharing them with others and me by e-mail, he quickly became one of my favorite authors.

I think you'll agree with me about his talent when you read about the varied experiences of this unique Aussie. From hilarious accounts related to sex education and burning toilet tissue to moving tributes to his dad and grandpa to touching stories about his own children, you'll laugh and cry at these episodes and their "Life Lessons."

And you'll get to know one remarkable guy, with the same kind of feelings, desires, and drives that we all have (or at least that the male of the species share), but with far more ability to express those feelings, and considerably more imagination, than most of us. And besides that, he's the father of two of the greatest grandchildren in the world!

The only thing I can't figure out is: How can one man have so many negative experiences with cats? Maybe he's a catalyst for catastrophic cat events.

Anyway, despite his feline failings, he does a great job at everything—including the writing of this book.

Yours,

Colonel Klink (aka Father-in-law Coy Roper)

P.S. Life Lesson No. 855: Always do a good job of choosing your sons-in-law.

Introduction

If your family is anything like mine, you probably have some wonderful storytellers who can make you laugh and make you cry. Such were my grandfathers, father, uncles and cousins. They could tell a yarn that would have you rolling in fits on the floor.

Invariably at the end of each story one of them would say, "You know what I learned from that?" Depending on the story being told, you might get any number of funny answers, like: someone holding up a hand with a missing finger and saying, "Never dare your sister to chop off your finger."

Those statements were a kind of roadmap that they were giving us. They were showing us the lessons that we could learn from the antics, actions or sad occasions that they had experienced. It was a kind of paternal advice that could be taken or ignored.

When the older members of our family passed away, I realized that we had lost a lot of those stories. No one had ever written them down. We could not remember all the details to recreate them. In essence that learned experience had died with them.

Thus I began to put together stories from my life for my children to keep and give to their children. As I said, some can be fairly funny; like the one with the advice that you should "never parachute your cat into a pack of wild dogs" or the one where I tell them "Don't set yourself on fire in the toilet stall." The telling of these two stories will have to wait until later. Some of our stories are sad and yet have a profound message that I want my children to remember. Most, however, are happy and reflect on the humorous side of family life.

We have also added special thoughts and prayers that were made on behalf of our family and children at the end of this book. These are added as guideposts to what our hopes and dreams are for their success, life, happiness, and most importantly their relationship with God.

Enjoy!

Life Lesson Number 1

—

"When you have to go, you have to go!"

When I was about three years old, Mum and Dad took me on a day trip into the big city of Sydney. I can't remember why we went to the city. I can't remember what we did in the city, but I can certainly remember what I did to my father on the way home from the city.

It was late in the afternoon and we were on one of the old brown single story train carriages that made up part of the train fleet of Sydney Rail. The carriage was packed with people and we could hardly move. Dad and Mum had negotiated their way into two seats at the end of the carriage that faced towards the center of the train allowing them to have the stroller in front of them. I of course, being the cute little precocious three-year-old, was entertaining the surrounding adults with cute smiles, sugar-doodles (summersaults to our American friends), and witty answers to simple questions.

One of the questions asked of me was, "What's your name little boy?" and I would answer, "Percy Pickles!" This name of course horrified the old lady that asked the question causing her to say "Oh, what a horrid name for such a cute little boy!" My Dad smiled at her response and I rolled around on the floor giggling to myself at the joke that I just played on the surrounding adults. Dad had a good sense of humor and he obviously liked me getting the attention. There is nothing like a proud father and son working the crowd together like this.

After a few sugar doodles, I stopped, stood up, turned to Dad and Mum and said, "I need to go

1

pooh!" Well nothing puts the old kybosh on a giggle session with adults more than the word "pooh" from a precocious three-year-old child. People began to avert their eyes and Dad began to get sweat beads on his forehead.

Why the sweat beads you might ask? Well, what I didn't know was that we were on an express train from Sydney to Granville and it only made one quick stop at a station called Strathfield. The problem was that we were almost there and the only way that I would be able to use the toilet was if we unloaded Mum, Dad, the stroller, and me, lost our prime seats, and had to wait for the all stations train to Granville later on in the afternoon.

Mum looked at Dad and she could see hesitation in his actions and thought processes. He was running down the Daddy list of things he would give up if he got off the train (like great seats and being home early to watch the cricket). She was running down the Mummy list of things she would have to do if I pooped my pants (like washing and scrubbing the clothes and having to harass Dad for letting it happen).

Needless to say, Dad would regret the indecision and the failure on his part to "Do the right thing." As the train screeched to a halt at Strathfield, Mum begged Dad to get off and take me to the toilet, but "No!" Dad sat there reasoning out loud that "I really didn't need to go and that I could make it home if I really wanted to!" If worst came to worst, Dad reasoned that me filling my pants would not be as bad as him getting home late and missing the end of the cricket. Mum just crossed her arms with disgust and waited for the inevitable.

Dad was wrong when he reasoned that at worst I would just fill my pants. While he was arguing with Mum about the situation and trying to get her to uncross her arms and help, I had stepped away from them, dropped my trousers and squatted on the floor of the train. The look of horror on the passengers' faces as this lovely little blond three-year-old boy took up the firing position was quite funny. When Dad realized what was going to happen, he looked at Mum (who just sat there with her arms crossed and her eyes burning holes in his forehead), looked back at me and started to say his first Daddy prayer. You know, the one that starts out, "Dear Lord, pleas don't let my son p...!" But it was too late.

I don't know what possessed Dad to do it, but he managed to whip out his best 2 shilling handkerchief, cover his cupped hands and catch the little message that his lovely son had so lovingly presented to everybody in that crowded carriage. Well, that was it. What can a father say in situations like that, "That's right, everybody look at me? I'm a self-centered idiot? I'm the one who put his own comfort ahead of his son's and now I'm the one paying for it!" He didn't have to say it, because everyone was thinking it. Mum just sat there looking on with amusement at the discomfort my father was in.

Having solved my problem, I arose, lifted my pants and went back to trying to entertain the masses with my jaunty wit and acrobatic antics. Dad of course knelt there with a lovely 2-shilling handkerchief full of pooh. The sweat beads dripped from the end of his nose. What to do, what to do? What he did not notice was that the entire end of the train carriage had begun to clear. Every passenger had had enough of the circus act before them and had begun to make their way through the crowded carriage to other carriages on the train. We were left alone, just the three of us in an empty carriage surrounded by train carriages crammed full of people like sardines in a tin can.

Dad stood up, opened the window, tossed his best handkerchief out the window, and sat down quietly on the train bench. He was as gray as a ghost. Mother just sat there smiling and she did not say a word.

So what did I learn from this experience?

1. The combination of the names "Percy" and "Pickles" has an interesting effect on old ladies.

2. When a three-year-old tells you he needs to go to the toilet now, he really means NOW!

3. Sugar Doodles and Fast Trains should never be combined.

4. Always keep a good handkerchief handy. You never know when you might need it.

5. The Daddy's prayer does not always work.

6. If you ever find yourself in a really crowded train and you want to get a good seat, then…nah! Who am I kidding? That would be too horrible a thought.

7. Dads, if you throw the "selfish/self-centered card" early in the game, don't expect Mum to throw the "Oh, let me help you out of this embarrassing situation" card when you need it.

Life Lesson Number 2

—

"Chocolate Coconut Balls!"

I spent the first five years of my life living at my Grandparents' house. My parents had built a small room on the back of their home and lived in this small extension until they could afford a home of their own. My grandparents were interesting people: hardworking, good-natured and very interested in their first grandchild, me.

In order to save time cutting the grass, my grandfather struck upon the idea of having a sheep live in the yard so that the grass could be naturally cut. After all, this was much better than pushing the rotary mower back and forth over the grass twice a week to keep it manageable.

My grandparents loved me. My parents loved me. Everybody loved me, and because they loved me they often bought me nice goodies to eat. My favorite was the chocolate coconut balls from the Darrel Lea chocolate shop. Second only to Rocky Road in my three-year-old estimation. It was this love of fine chocolate that got me into trouble.

I can remember being fascinated by the sheep in our yard. Not just because it was big and wooly and was somewhat frightened by a three-year-old, but because it ate grass, drank water, and produced (what appeared to be) "chocolate coconut balls." Under constant grandparent or parent supervision, I had been curtailed in my fascination for this wondrous production process. My grandfather collected all the "wondrous chocolate coconut balls" daily, thus depriving me of any chance of enjoying my favorite treats. I needed a plan.

Each day Nana would sit with me while we watched the Mickey Mouse show on the black and white television. She quite often took a nap while I sat there dutifully singing along and enjoying the show. It was during one of these naps that I made my break for the backyard.

I approached the sheep carefully, reached down and tore out a large handful of grass. I quickly popped it in my mouth and munched away. "Yuck!" it was terri-

4

ble. I guess that the sheep had some special process whereby it could change this green foul tasting grassy stuff into chocolate. Well, the main course behind me, I was now on to the dessert portion of this experiment.

I knew that my grandfather would collect and keep all this chocolate for himself, so I began my collection and planned a hiding place so that I could have all the chocolate that I wanted later. It was during this gathering process that Nana stepped out the back door and yelled at me. Why? I don't know. I guess she thought that I was stealing all my Grandfather's chocolate.

Even a three-year-old knows when the gig is up. I knew that the chocolate balls were going to be confiscated and that I would be in trouble. I figured, "In for a penny, in for a pound," so I popped one of those lovely chocolates into my mouth so Nana wouldn't get them all. Funny thing, it tasted nothing like the chocolate that I was used to!

So what have I learned from this experience?

1. If you steal your grandfather's chocolate coconut balls, you get into big trouble.

2. You can get your mouth washed out with soap for doing things other than saying bad words.

3. Stay inside on mowing day. Grandfathers get grumpy if they have to go back to push mowing the lawn.

4. Even a three-year-old gets tired of lamb chops after a few weeks.

5. No matter how hard you look, sometimes you never find where grandfather hides his chocolate coconut ball stash.

Life Lesson Number 3

—

"Fire Bad!"

In Australia we celebrated the Queen's Birthday with what we called "Cracker Night." This was the one day each year when we could set off fireworks (crackers) in celebration of the Queen's long life. Preparation for this day started almost a week in advance. We began to collect old wood and bits of garbage that we could build a bonfire with. On Cracker Night we would light the bonfire, throw some meat on the barbeque and let off the firecrackers that we had bought.

At five years old, this would be my first memorable cracker night. I had been instrumental in collecting and piling all the burnable garbage and wood on to the bonfire pile in the back yard. It grew larger each day as grandparents, parents and neighbors offered pieces of cardboard, wood and old furniture to get the celebration going. Since I had such an integral part in the building of this bonfire, I assumed ownership of its shape, size and contents. I finally deemed that the bonfire pyre was finished and that it was ready to go.

Five-year-olds tend to have a different sense of time than adults. To me the bonfire was finished and ready to go, and yet it was still several days until the Queen's Birthday holiday. After two days of complaining about waiting until the holiday I struck upon a plan to get the fire going on my schedule. All I needed was a method to light the bonfire.

My first attempt was somewhat simple. I had taken a newspaper and rolled it into a torch-like object and tried to find a place where I could light it with fire. I noticed that Nana had the electric heater on in the lounge room to keep the room warm. To me, this was the obvious place to light the rolled paper. I planned to then take the lit torch through the kitchen, down the hall, through the laundry, out the backdoor, across the yard and set the bonfire raging. Who cared if I was the only one there to see it burn; after all, it was my bonfire.

I waited patiently until Nana had left the lounge room and made my way to the heater, stuck in the paper torch and laughed with glee as the papers burst into flame. I was off to a good start. I turned and began to carry the torch like a true Olympian. My form was true with the torch held aloft as I valiantly ran on to my goal. Unfortunately, as I turned through the kitchen, the burned papers were starting to peel off and waft back down on to me.

I made it halfway down the hallway before Nana heard my yells of pain and rescued me. She grabbed the lit torch, rushed to the kitchen sink and put it out under a torrent of water. My Nana was a very patient person, but this event tested her to her limits. I new that I was in big trouble and that I would have some explaining to do when my parents and grandfather came home. Nana unplugged the heater and stashed it away out of my reach. I was dejected and down, but not out. Nana tended the small burned spots on my arm as I sat quietly dejected.

As five-year-old logic would have it, I determined that if that bonfire was going to be lit, it had to be lit before the parents and grandfather came home. Surely, they would dismantle the object as punishment for me and I would never again have a bonfire of my own to light. While sitting in the kitchen waiting for my fate to play out, I noticed something that I had missed before.

My grandfather had smoked a pipe for many years. All his pipe equipment, including a cigarette lighter, was on the cabinet beside his collection of pipes and tobacco. This would be my method of ignition. While Nana wasn't looking I snuck over, grabbed the lighter and sat back down. While this was a good way to light a fire, I had had no experience with trying to actually light a fire using a lighter. I needed to practice, but I needed a place where Nana couldn't see me. Where could that be?

My grandparents had recently purchased large armchairs and couches for the living room. These pieces were high enough off the ground to slide under (where I could not be seen) and there practice the art of lighting a cigarette lighter. I had to hurry, grandfather would be home any minute. So I made my move. I slipped off the chair and under the couch.

I can remember smiling to myself at how smart I was to outwit the adults around me. I began working with the lighter. Clicking, spinning, and thumbing the starter, but to no avail. I had watched my grandfather do it many times, and if he could do it, so could I. Just then I heard his voice in the hallway as Nana introduced to him my antics of the day. It was now or never. I took one last flick of my thumb over the lighter and "WHOOSH" that lovely blue flame came shooting out the top lighter setting the Hessian or Burlap under the couch on fire. Smoke and burning particles began to bellow out from under the couch where two little legs were sticking out.

Once again I gave myself away as I screamed for help. How was I to know that fire could take hold that quickly? Thank goodness, Grandfather was there to drag me out from under the couch, flip it over and beat out the flames with a lovely cushion that Nana had made. Needless to say, I never did get to light my bonfire. Come to think of it, grandfather never smoked again after that day.

So what have I learned from this experience?

1. Fire is "Bad!"

2. Boys who play with fire are "Bad!"

3. The distance a five-year-old can carry a flaming roll of paper is inversely proportional to the size of the flame.

4. All cigarette lighters are not child proof.

5. Hessian flares up like wafer thin toilet paper when exposed to an open flame.

6. Grandfathers are grumpy when they are not allowed to smoke anymore.

Life Lesson Number 4

—

"Confirmation—Girls hate me"

Catholic girls have no sense of humor. You know how I know? I know because two of the meanest Catholic girls on my Nana's street beat me up as a child. I can remember looking up at them from the ground with a huge green snot bubble billowing from my nose. Their curly brown locks of hair dangled towards my tear covered face as they leaned in to shake their fists at me one last time, shouting: "…and if you ever do that again! You will get worse next time!"

I knew they were serious. I had no doubt that they were capable of making my life miserable. I was a small but stocky five-year-old who had just been taken out by a couple of "girls." Life was not looking up for me.

As they walked away, I continued to lie there thinking that any movement at all would entice them to come back and finish the job. I did manage to turn my head to the right and notice my green water pistol smashed into a thousand sharp plastic pieces beside me. Tears welled up in my eyes at this added injustice.

What had I done to deserve this? I had just received that beautiful green water pistol the day before as a gift from my grandfather. I took great pride in learning how to load it from the tap in the laundry and then chase people around and shoot them. Well, "people" actually meant my grandmother and grandfather, and being older they soon became tired of the game. So, I needed to find myself another target.

While sitting cross-legged in the back yard of my Nana's house shooting at bugs and ants, I noticed a constant stream of young girls dressed in beautiful white confirmation dresses heading off down to the Catholic Church for some function or other. I said to myself, "You know what would be fun? How about I shoot some of those girls with my water pistol when they are on their way back home!" I had a plan.

The waiting was intense. I had filled my water pistol and sat cross-legged up against the paling fence not more than three feet from where the girls would pass.

I reasoned that I could shoot them and then turn and run before they would even know what happened. I waited, and while I waited I began to wonder, "What if I shoot them and they don't realize that they have been shot by a water pistol!" That would be bad. The whole ambush thing would have gone to waste.

I needed something to ensure that those girls "knew" that they had been shot by the best water pistol marksman on the street. Then it hit me. What I needed was "Muddy Water." With muddy water the shots would show up on the lovely white starched dresses and they would notice, laugh and say, "Hey, you really got us, didn't you!" All the while marveling at my marksmanship. My place would be secured in history as the best shot on the street.

You might think that loading a water pistol with muddy water is hard. It's not for a five-year-old on a mission. You just mix dirt and water in a cup; scoop out the "floaters" and pour that brown concoction into the water pistol. I was locked and loaded. Nothing could go wrong. I was ready.

Perhaps I should have been more choosey about my targets. I could hear them coming up the path giggling away and talking about girl stuff. At the right moment I jumped up, took aim and leveled a volley of shots right at both of their midsections. Patton would have been proud of the planning and implementation of this ambush.

I stood there smiling, waiting for the two girls to break down laughing at being caught off guard. It was then that I noticed that these two girls were about nine or ten years old. They were twice my size, and although dressed like little white angels, had the temperament of two bobcats in a gunnysack fighting over a morsel of meat and "I was about to be that meat." A shiver ran up my spine as I realized that I was the only one enjoying this little prank. I assumed the Wiley Coyote pose as I turned to run away, but it was too late.

To cut a long story short, both girls jumped the fence in a one-handed leap, grabbed me by the shirt as my little feet ran out from under me and proceeded to slap me about the head and shoulders until I collapsed on the ground. Through the whole beating they were screaming, "Look what you've done to our dresses!" It was somewhere in this wild melee that one of them took my water pistol and crushed it under foot.

So there you have it. A grave injustice had been done. I had attempted to brighten the day of a few Catholic girls and this is the thanks I get. I would show them. I would tell my grandparents what they did to me and then…then! Then it hit me. I couldn't tell a single soul. What self-respecting five-year-old would get beaten up by two Catholic girls in confirmation dresses and talk about it? I could tell no one.

So what have I learned from this experience?

1. Catholic girls have no sense of humor.

2. Fences don't always make for good neighbors; in fact they hardly slow their kids down.

3. Choosing the right target is more important than hitting the target.

4. Timing is everything when it comes to your escape plan.

5. You can literally get the snot beat out of you.

Life Lesson Number 5

—

"Trajectory and Murphy's Law"

Five-year-olds often find themselves with lots of time on their hands. That is a bad thing. Given enough time, these innocent little imps can turn a harmless pastime into a near catastrophic event. Such was the case in what I would always remember as "The Clay Tennis Court Incident."

Two doors up from my Nana's house there was an old dilapidated orange clay tennis court. It was worn to the point that it was hardly ever used for tennis anymore. It was, however, a great place for kids to play off the street, out of sight of their parents/grandparents, and out of mind.

It had rained for several days and the court was a wonderful quagmire of oozy orange clay. It was marvelous for making wonderful fist-sized mud pies. Mark, my best friend and cohort in crime, suggested that he and I make a bunch of them and store them at the front paling fence at the edge of the tennis court.

I can honestly say that when we set out we were only intent on "accumulating" mud pies at the front fence. I did not realize that once we had "accumulated" these mud pies that idle minds might begin to question, "What should be done with them?" The answer became obvious. The Catholic girls were walking home from school again. Target acquired.

I can remember the mischievous look that Mark gave me as we both realized at the same time that this was the chance to get back at these girls for "the water pistol incident." (Ok, I did confide in him how the girls had beaten me up. He was my best friend after all.) So we hauled back, lobbed two great big mud pies over the tennis court fence and waited for the screams.

We missed the girls by a few feet, but we were close enough to scare them into a dead run. Boy, were we ecstatic—we had lobbed the mud pies, scared the girls to death and not even been detected. It couldn't get any better than this. Or could it!

I picked up the biggest mud pie that I could find and waited for my next target. The pie was wet and juicy and barely holding together. It would prove to be the best splattering mud pie that we had ever seen. Just then, the dry cleaning man's van pulled into the street. His little van had a sliding door on the side that he kept open as he delivered from house to house. This was it. Here was our target. What were the chances, after all, of a five-year-old hitting a moving van with a mud pie? I hauled back and threw.

Little did I know that the van driver would actually see the pie as it was lobbed at his van and STOP just in case it did some damage and he lose control of his vehicle. This had the effect of presenting a stationary target for the final trajectory stage of the pie's descent; straight through the open side door, and all over the dry cleaning in the van.

When I realized that I had actually hit the dry cleaning in the van, I jumped up on the fence and yelled, "We're sorry mister, we didn't mean to hit you!" This was a mistake. I had given away our position. What followed was reminiscent of a Keystone Cops episode.

The driver abandoned his van in the middle of the road, dove out the left side, grabbed a rolled up newspaper off the sidewalk and took off after us. Mark and I took one look at each other and took off through the tennis court.

Now, you may think that a five-year-old chubby kid is not quick on his feet, but let me tell you we kept a good distance between the van man and our heels. To add to the possibility of escape, Mark had quickly climbed over one paling fence after another. I had followed. After each fence I looked back to see the Van driver panting and losing ground as he climbed fences. I kept yelling at him to forgive us. He just waved the paper at me screaming, "When I get hold of you, you're done for!"

We finally reached a point where Mark suggested we go to ground. So we picked a yard, clambered up under the foundations of the house and hid quietly in the dark recesses of the foundation. After a few minutes we could see the legs of the van man walking through the yard, rolled up paper in hand dangling at his side. We were dead for sure.

Just then the lady of the house burst out the back door asking what the man was doing there in her yard. After he made a feeble attempt to explain that he was after two criminals, she shooed him off and he left. Under that house, the sweat beads ran down our foreheads and dripped off our noses. We were safe, at least for now.

Just to be sure we waited another hour before sneaking out and running home to Nana's place. The whole time we were under that house, we were sure that we could hear that little van driving back and forth through the neighborhood look-ing for us.

From that day on I dove for cover each time I heard a knock on the door and a voice calling, "Dry Cleaning Delivery!"

So what have I learned from this experience?

1. Catholic girls are mean, but they scare easy.

2. Fences sure do slow down old people who are chasing you.

3. Five-year-olds innately have the feral ability to scale fences of any height.

4. Always remove rolled up newspapers from the sidewalk before you do some-thing stupid.

5. Never assume that you will MISS something that you are aiming for.

6. Hiding under the bed each time the dry cleaning man makes a delivery is hard to explain to your Nana.

Life Lesson Number 6

—

"Cracker Night"

For a young boy, cracker night is never really over. You always hide away a small stash of crackers that can be used at a later date to "blow up" things that, well, just need blowing up.

Such was the case one-day after my seventh cracker night. I was visiting at my grandparents' house and had a pocket full of Tom Thumb crackers as well as a box of matches. I kept telling myself that this would be great. There were always good things to blow up at Nana's house.

Now I know what you're thinking: this kid is a nightmare. But I wasn't really destructive. I mostly blew up ant holes (with maybe a few ant casualties), garden dirt, the occasional snail or if luck had it, a tin can. I was on a roll this day. I had worked my way down my list of things to "blow up" and yet I still had one more Tom Thumb to light. What to do? What to do?

Just then, a rather large dog deposited a large stinky pile of dog poop on the grass strip just outside the front gate. To others this would have been something so totally disgusting that they would have turned their backs and shunned the steaming vision like the plague. To a seven-year-old boy this was a gift from heaven. I said to myself, "Someone could step in that." I stood there mesmerized as I went over the logistics of what was about to happen. I had been presented with the ultimate Tom Thumb test. Could I completely obliterate a dog poop with one cracker and save some poor unsuspecting person from a shoe full of poop?

With my last Tom Thumb in one hand and my matches in the other, I approached the steaming pile. I slowly knelt down beside this test of my explosive skills, and like a bomb disposal expert trying to defuse a dangerous situation, gingerly poked my Tom Thumb into the center of the pile. I carefully gauged the depth to which it should be inserted. I needed to assure that there would be complete obliteration, no remnant left to cause concern. Having achieved the required depth I leaned back, smiled at my handiwork, and wondered how funny this would be if the poop were to explode over some poor innocent passerby. I shook my head, no, even that was *too horrible* to think of. I pulled the wick upright, reached for my matches, knelt on one knee and struck the match.

Now, if you have ever played with crackers you will know that some types of wicks burn quickly and some slowly. It has something to do with how tightly the wick is packed with gunpowder. In most cases, the tightly packed wicks will burn slowly and systematically giving the user a good six to ten seconds to run away and take cover. Such had been the case for every other Tom Thumb in my stash. I definitely had six to ten seconds to make my getaway through the fence and to safety.

What happened next, happened in slow motion. I touched the match to the wick, saw it flash (I smiled and told myself that this was a good wick), but then sputter…sputter…thwwt. "No!" I screamed loudly. During the sputter phase I had assumed the pose of Wiley E Coyote as he tries to run away in one direction but his face remains behind frozen in time. It was too late. I had two to three seconds, tops, before the Tom Thumb exploded.

I stood there in that stupid cartoon pose for a few moments trying to take in what had just happened, eyes clenched tight, feeling the spray stuck all over me like a bad case of dog poop freckles. I opened one eye, looked back at the ground where the time bomb had once been, pumped my fist and yelled, "Yes! I did it!" The poop was completely gone. The Tom Thumb had completely obliterated the steaming dog poop and had blown ninety percent of it all over me.

So what have I learned from this experience?

1. With a little work you can "join wicks together" to give you more time to escape.

2. Explosives and young boys should be closely supervised.

3. Dog poop can travel at twice the speed of a seven-year-old.

4. It takes three days before your mother smells the clothes hidden under your mattress.

5. Always, I repeat, always keep your mouth closed in disposal operations like this.

Life Lesson Number 7

—

"Why Cats hate me"

Whoever said that an idle mind is the devil's playground was probably referring to the mind of a five-year-old boy. Well, maybe not all five-year-old boys, but maybe just to me. My active little mind always sought a solution to problems that I faced. What was today's problem? My kitten did not want to be carried around and I was bored.

In general, cats are pretty docile creatures and do enjoy a little attention every now and then. Unfortunately my cat had been getting "attention" all day. I had played soccer with it. It would not kick the ball back to me after the ball knocked him over. I had tried to teach the kitten how to swim. That did not go well. The kitten would also not fit inside my small car garage no matter how hard I pushed him. Needless to say, the kitten's nerves were shot.

I had taken to carrying him around in a headlock. Why? Because every time I tried to put him down he ran away. If I tried to carry him in my hands he would try to wiggle loose. So the headlock it was. It is quite a sight to see a little kitten head poking out from under someone's armpit. From the rear you could see the little kitten pushing for all it was worth with its feet, trying to set itself free from this malodorous situation.

The morning had essentially fallen apart for me. My Grandmother was angry because she found the kitten swinging by its tail from the rotary clothesline at the end of a piece of string. How could that happen?

It was simple. I needed to tie the kitten up so that it would not run away. Why the tail, you might ask? I say, why not the tail? It was as good as any place to tie a piece of string. Why was the cat airborne, you might ask? Well, it didn't actually start out airborne; it just "accidentally" ended up that way.

After coming up with the bright idea of tying up the cat, I had found enough string in the shed to solve the problem. I threw the string over the clothesline and tied it to the cat's tail. The cat seemed perfectly happy to be away from me and at least temporarily left alone. I smiled as I watched it walk around pulling the clothesline a little as it went.

Then without warning the wind kicked up and caught some of my Grandmother's washing on the line. The line swung around and "there it was"—a new diversion. When the wind blew, the clothesline moved, pulling the cat off the ground. This caused a funny howl to come from the little kitten. This was pretty funny to a five-year-old with time on his hands and without warning the "what ifs" started bouncing around inside in my head. "What if I cranked the clothesline up and spun it around myself? The cat would make that noise again, wouldn't it?" I said to myself. I started to set my plan in motion, but it was as I was cranking up the line that my Grandmother came out the back door and put the whole thing to rest. With that diversion gone, I would need something else to do.

With the kitten under my arm I set off for the front porch to sit and contemplate what to do next. I was bored, the kitten was irate, and my Grandmother seemed relieved that I had given up on my first intent. As I sat up on the brick wall of the front porch several small dogs made their way down the street in a pack. As they passed by the open front gate, they sensed the kitten and ran barking to the bottom of the brick porch.

As I sat on the bricks, I judged that the dogs could not reach us where we were. They barked and jumped trying to get to the kitten, which I held securely under my armpit. I thought it was really funny how they wailed as I leaned over to look at them. Then it struck me: they were after the kitten. So I took the kitten out and holding it in two hands held it out over the dogs. The dogs went wild, the kitten hissed and wailed, and I giggled.

When I brought the cat back over the porch, the dogs quieted down. When I stuck the kitten out they would go wild. This was great. For several minutes I went through the "Kitten out, Kitten in, Kitten out, Kitten in" movements until I was tired of it. The kitten actually looked relieved to take up his position under my armpit. Wait a minute. I was bored again!

What could I do now that might amuse me? I checked my pockets, found a handkerchief in one and some string in the other. It didn't take long for a kid who liked to play "war" to figure out that the "101st Airborne Cat Brigade" was about to drop into Normandy to face the hostile "Hounds." After a few minutes I had fashioned the parachute and positioned myself high over the drop zone. As jumpmaster on this trip I made sure that I held our troops way out high over the Hounds and let him go.

The chute only partially deployed on Lieutenant Kitten but it did actually slow his descent enough that the kitten was not hurt as it landed amidst the Hounds. I had prepared myself for the possibility of casualties but did not expect what I saw. Instead of running away from the dogs, the kitten was now trying to jump back up onto the ledge where I was sitting. He would have made it too, had his little drogue chute not slowed his ascent down each time. From the air it looked like a wild melee of hounds throwing a bug eyed cat wearing a parachute back up at me. After four or five attempts at the jump the kitten finally decided to make his escape into the back yard. The dogs followed nipping at the billowing handkerchief. Fortunately, the kitten made it to safety without a scratch on him. Unfortunately, I can't say the same for any mental scars on the poor little thing. Life was good. From a five-year-olds perspective, my work here was done and my day was complete. My grandmother and her frazzled nerves could finally rest.

So what have I learned from this experience?

1. Cats don't like me.

2. After this incident, you never could find string at Grandmother's house.

3. Cats don't like scuba diving in the bathtub.

4. Cats can't play soccer.

5. Cats don't like dogs.

6. You can't stuff a round cat into a square hole.

7. You can parachute a cat into a pack of wild dogs, but the cat really doesn't like it.

8. Grandmothers are the most patient people in the world.

9. Cats do have nine lives. They just use them up quicker around me.

10. Give me a roll of duct tape, a Leatherman tool, three snickers, and ten bored five-year-olds and I could take over a small country.

11. Grandmothers never tell your parents the really bad things that you do.

Life Lesson Number 8

—

"That won't fit in there, Cliff!"

My Dad had been summoned up to the farm by has father (who was getting on in years at the time). My mother and I accompanied him up to the farm to see what Fardie Shep wanted. (Fardie was my loving childhood name for my grandfather. It is equivalent to the American Pee Paw, only much crueler and funnier).

On arrival, Fardie came out with the shotgun and said, "Cliff, the draft horse has had it. She's all played out and I don't want to waste money on her with the Vet. Take her down the lower end of the paddock and shoot her." Dad, being the obedient son, grabbed the gun and started off down towards the barn. He did not question his father at all. He did, however, eye my mother to see what her reaction was to this request. She was not pleased. She liked the horse, as it had become a favorite of mine.

Dad knew what had to be done. He stopped by the barn and grabbed a bunch of tools that he would need to dig the hole to bury the horse, leaned them over his shoulder and set off to select a spot for the interment. Having found a nice soft piece of ground (he was thinking ahead), he laid down the tools and shotgun and went off in search of the horse.

Old Bess had been a good horse. She had worked the farm for years. She was almost as large as the Clydesdales that pull the Anhauser-Bush Beer wagon. Dad led her down to the spot that he wanted, stood her just a few feet uphill of the soft spot, patted her on the forehead, stepped back, raised the gun, and dropped her dead with one shot between the eyes. He did not flinch from the task.

Mum was not impressed. The efficiency with which Dad had dropped the old horse gave my mother the willies; so she set off up to the house for a while to rest while Dad dug the hole.

After about an hour she went back down to check on how Dad was going. Dad stood in a hole about three feet wide, five feet long and about five feet deep.

He could see the puzzled look on her face as she walked up. At first Mum didn't say anything, but then curiosity got the better of her.

She said, "Cliff, that hole is not big enough to hold that horse!" Dad ignored her. "Cliff, you'll have to make that hole a lot bigger than that. The horse won't fit!" Dad looked at her and said, "Don't worry about it, Audrey; the horse will fit!"

This back and forth went on with my Dad hoping beyond hope that Mum would just "go away" and let him finish. But she was a persistent one. She stayed until Dad finally climbed out of the hole.

The back and forth continued: "Cliff, we'll be here all day unless you dig that hole bigger! It's legs and head won't fit in!" Dad tried one more time to convince her by saying, "Audrey, the horse will fit, just go on up to the house!"

At this point Dad realized that to continue to argue with her would be useless. Mum started up again, "Cliff, get someone to help you or you will never get the hole dug big enough to get that…that…that…!" Her words trailed off as she realized what was happening.

While she was talking, Dad turned away from her, bent over and picked up his woodman axe. It was the one that he used to use when he did competition wood chopping. "It WILL fit, Audrey!" he said as he turned back around. But no one was there to hear him. There was just a cloud of dust heading up the hill to the farmhouse.

Dad was right. The horse did fit in that little hole, and with room to spare!

So what have I learned from this experience?

1. Conservation of energy comes naturally to farmers. "Yeah sure, we could dig a big hole…but…that would be work!"

2. When it comes to digging dirt, the smaller the hole and sharper the axe the better.

3. Mothers sometimes don't think outside the box.

4. Fathers just want to stuff the box full and bury it.

5. I wonder if Mother ever worried about growing old and feeble with a man who could shoot, dismember, and bury a lifelong friend the moment it got sick.

6.   Check the boot (trunk) of the car for "burying" tools if Dad ever offers to take you to the doctor.

7.   Never let it be said that my Dad COULD NOT put a square plug in a round hole. He would just shave off the sides and make it fit.

(Here is a picture of Dad, the horse and me in the field where the horse was eventually buried.)

Life Lesson Number 9

—

"Mabel's Embarrassing Moment"

When Dad was a young lad he attended a small church of Christ in the mountains at Kurrajong. He told us the story many times of how the preacher there would always encourage people in the community to come to church. While walking through the town one day, the preacher ran into Old Tom from a farm off the Burlisson Rd a few miles out of the tiny little town. The preacher knew that Old Tom had never darkened the door of any church let alone his church. Not being put off by Tom's lack of interest, the preacher struck up a conversation with old Tom.

Now, Tom was a bit deaf. Well, to tell you the truth, he was as deaf as a post, but he could hear enough to carry on a conversation if you were up close to him. The preacher approached him and invited him to come to church next Sunday. Old Tom shook his head and said, "I don't have a need for that sort of thing!", and started to set off down the street bidding the preacher a good day.

As Tom walked off, the preacher said loudly, "If there is ever anything that I can do for you, just let me know?" Old Tom stopped, turned and putting his finger to the side of his head said, "Well, to tell you the truth, my old cow Mabel has gone missing. Could you announce that to your congregation and have them let me know if they see her?" The preacher listened to Tom's description of Mabel and agreed to make the announcement that next Sunday.

When Sunday came around, the preacher was up making the announcements when he noticed that Old Tom had slipped into the back of the small church building. He had sat himself on the back row and was sitting there holding his hand up to his ear trying to hear what was going on.

As the preacher started through his announcements he tried to talk loud enough so that Old Tom could hear him.

"We're glad that the Smith Family has made it back safely from their trip to Sydney and it's good to see all the children sitting on the front row. In other announcements, sister Mabel has not been feeling well and asks for our prayers. She has been having arthritis trouble and has found it hard to get out."

Old Tom had been listening intently from the back of the building. All he heard in that announcement were the words "Mabel" and "get out." When he saw that the audience didn't react to what the preacher said, Old Tom stood up, raised his hand to get attention, and at the top of his voice said, "Did you tell them that Mabel has a brown spot on her offside hip and a dummy tit?"

Well, with that little clarification the audience broke down into fits of laughter, thus offending old Tom. He left that little building, never to darken the door of any church in town again. As for poor Sister Mabel and her arthritis, people at that church and in that town never looked at her the same way again.

So what have I learned from this experience?

1. Always listen closely in church.

2. Never assume that you heard what you think you heard.

3. Never assume that what you said was what was heard.

4. A stigma can be attached to your person without you even being present, and it can last for a lifetime. Wait, it has actually lasted past Mabel's lifetime.

5. I have figured out the brown spot thing, but I have no idea what a dummy tit is?

Life Lesson Number 20

—

"When you're dead, you're really dead!"

He reached into his pockets and pulled out his first pension check. Showing it to his son, he said, "For the first time in sixty-five years we will be on easy street, Cliff! We have been battling on this farm for all these years with nothing. Now we have the farm and extra income to get by on." He was proud of having made it those many years without being a burden to anyone and now he was ready to reap the rewards of a long hard life.

A few days later he and Ina were making their way through the bean fields. The green plants stood tall around him as he made his way towards the barbwire fence to head back to the house. It had been a hard day's work for him. He still had the un-cashed pension check in his pocket. As he bent to climb through the barbwire fence he stumbled and fell, grasping his chest. Ina didn't notice that he had fallen at first, but then turning to see why Cecil didn't answer her questions, she found him lying dead of a massive heart attack at the age of sixty five. He never got to cash the check that would make life so much easier.

I didn't understand what was wrong. All I knew was that Mum and Dad had stopped to pick me up in the Morris Minor as I walked home from school. They had never come by car to pick me up from school. This was most unusual. Mum was crying and Dad was as gray as a ghost. Finally, after pleading with them both to tell me what was wrong, Mum told me that Fardie Shep had died and that we were on our way up to the farm to help Nana get ready for the funeral. I had never had anyone die on me before. I couldn't understand what it was all about. I sat quietly in the back of the car as we headed off to the farm.

Farmers are self-sufficient in almost everything. They birth their children at home. They grow their children on the farm and they feed their children from the farm. As adults they made their living off the farm and the animals the farm produced. Even in death this proud band of people took care of their own, down on the farm.

After the doctor had come by to sign the death certificate, the death ritual began at the farmhouse. By the time I arrived, the nurse had been and had cleaned up the body and had dressed Fardie Shep in his Sunday best, ready for the funeral. Fardie was laid out in the spare bedroom out the back off the porch room. His hair was combed and he had been shaved (which was quite unusual for my grandfather). People were milling around everywhere. Many visitors came and went, leaving food and drinks for the family.

Family members that lived nearby were arriving to greet the guests and take condolences from the visitors as they said goodbye to Fardie. It was all quite a show for a 6-year-old boy. I had never in my life seen a dead person before and I had no idea what an impact that would have on my life for the next several years to come.

I had indicated that I didn't want to see my grandfather and that I was afraid to go up to him. My parents thought that was okay, but my grandmother thought that I needed to say goodbye. Having made this decision for me, she dragged me into the room, took my hand and ran my fingers through his hair and told me how natural he looked. "Natural", I thought to myself, "This guy is dead." Then my active little mind went into overdrive and I started to think of questions and consequences. "Wait a minute," I thought to myself, "If he can die, so can I, and so can my mother and father!" This is not good. For the first time I realized that I was mortal and that someday soon Mum and Dad would both die as well.

When it came time for the funeral, the undertaker showed up with the coffin. He needed some help getting it into the house, so Dad and the sons-in-law helped get the coffin into the bedroom. Not one to shrink from any task, Dad put his father in the coffin and laid him out nicely prior to closing the lid for the last time. I was mortified. When you die, they seal you in a box and bury you under the ground. I closed my eyes and imagined what it would be like to find myself in a box. Not good again. This dying was a bad thing.

The church service was short and sweet. It was held at the Kurrajong Church of Christ. All the family were there and neighbors and friends came from all over the shire. The one song I do remember them singing was "In the sweet by and by." To this day that song takes me back to Fardie's funeral and brings a tear to my eye. My mother cried through the whole funeral. She really liked Cecil and she knew that his passing would leave a huge gap in Dad's life as they had gotten on so well together. She also cried for the lost special relationship that Cecil had with the only grandchild that would carry on his Shepherd name.

When it came time to bury Fardie at North Richmond cemetery, Mum decided that it would all be too much for me. She was right. Even the sight of them lowering the coffin into the grave from a distance disturbed me. After the funeral people went back to the farmhouse for tea and biscuits.

The next few weeks were very hard for me. I had never had anyone die on me prior to this time. I had always been a good student and I loved going to school. But things had changed. On the first day of school after the funeral, I dragged around the house as Mum tried to get me ready. I feigned sickness, but that did not work. She made me get dressed, made my lunch, and sent me off out the door with a kiss. I went around the corner of the house and stood there. Mum must have been watching for me to go down the street because when I didn't appear she came out to see what I was doing. I'll tell you what I was doing. I was reasoning that if I left Mum at home on her own that she would die and that I would have to bury her. If I did not leave, she would not die. This was a good plan.

Initially Mum tried to find out what was wrong with me. I refused to tell her why I wouldn't move and only that I was not going to school, ever again. Well, this just made Mum angry at me. She went back inside, reached over the door and got the Kewpie doll stick down. When she came back outside I knew I was in trouble, so I would run twenty or thirty yards and stop, keeping just out of her reach. It was a vicious cycle. Mum would catch up to me; I would run another twenty yards and stop and the whole process would start again. Not the most ideal situation for a kid that was supposed to be on his way to school, but at least I could see Mum, and if I could see her then she wouldn't die.

This cycle went on for weeks. Mum would literally have to chase me to school with the Kewpie doll stick to get me to go. When school got out, I ran as fast as I could home to make sure she was still alive. After about a month of finding her okay, I started to relax and go to school on my own again.

It wasn't until a visit home from America in the late 1990's that I told Mum the reason why I wouldn't go to school. When I did tell her, she felt terrible for having chased me with the stick all the way to school. She just thought that I was being a stubborn little boy. Little did she know that by my keeping her within eyesight, I was doing her a great favor, I was keeping her alive.

So what have I learned from this experience?

1. When you're dead, you're dead.

2. There are no degrees of death.

3. Death rituals should be carefully explained to small children.

4. Regardless of what Nana tells you, there is no such thing as "looking natural" when you're dead. You just look dead.

5. When you get that first pension check, cash it quickly.

6. Being good and working hard doesn't guarantee a long life.

7. You should always hide the kewpie doll stick if you're going to be bad.

8. You should never wait thirty years to tell the truth about something you did.

9. Just being able to "see someone" will not keep her alive. It just makes you feel better.

Life Lesson number 25

—

"The Morris Minor"

The first car that Dad every bought for himself was a Morris Minor. It was a tiny dark gray British car that had a small four-cylinder engine and barely enough room for Dad, Mum, and me. It had a four speed floor shift gear change, no seat belts, and little flipper lights that would flip out from the door jams to indicate if you were turning left or right. It wasn't new and it wasn't pretty, but it was Dad's pride and joy. Unfortunately, I developed a fascination for this car that was only equaled by my fascination with cats.

It seemed that almost each time I got into that car something happened. First, I was not a good car traveler so on any trip of more than a few minutes I would hurl everywhere over the lovely vinyl seats and floor mats. This frustrated my father no end. He could not understand how anyone could get sick in a car after only a few minutes. His frustration didn't change anything. I would just hurl. Dad finally carried something for me to throw up in that he could empty at the petrol stations we so frequently had to stop at.

It was during one of these frequent stops at a petrol station that Dad looked over at me and said, "Son, stay in the car. I am emptying the puke pot and filling the tank, so don't get out!" Well, being the good son that I am, I sat there for all of two more minutes before the need to get out and see what was going on at the petrol pump overcame me. Instead of getting out Dad's door, I swung open the door beside me with my foot, pushing it its full length out into the lane next to us. This foot push was met by an EJ Holden screaming in to the pump next to us and tearing off the little Morris Minor door. Oops! I was in big trouble. It was apparently all my fault. No one even questioned the bozo that sped into the pump at great speed and almost squished me as I was getting out. Dad had to buy a second hand door (which was a different gray color) and put it on the car. It never looked the same after that.

A few weeks later I was sitting in the back of the car when my Dad ran over a large bump on Flushcombe Road near South Blacktown School. It was a notoriously large bump that could cause the car to almost go airborne if you forgot it was there. Well, Dad forgot it was there and as we left the ground, my head went through the roof of the car. Thank goodness the metal shell stopped me from being launched into space, but my great huge noggin tore a massive hole in the roof upholstery that Dad had to fix with the early equivalent of duct tape. It was just another annoying blemish on the car that Dad had always wanted.

Another time Dad asked me to stay in the car while we were up at the farm. He said that he would only be a few minutes and that I should not touch anything. Well, to a young fellow with nothing to do, that was a fate worse than death. I took it upon myself to practice changing gears at great speed. This of course, was all accomplished from the other side of the driver's seat where there is no clutch to depress. It took three hours and a mechanic to come and reconnect the gear change mechanisms so that we could head off for home. Dad never did figure out that I had exercised my special attention on the gearbox while he was gone. He just thought it was a touch of bad luck. He was half right. I was bad luck and I had touched his gearbox.

The final episode with our Morris Minor came when we were on our way back home from a holiday at Nowra down the south coast. We had to drive the poor little Morris back up an extremely steep hill called Bulli Pass. Halfway up that hill the poor little motor gave out and died. Now wait a minute! I had nothing to do with the motor blowing up. What was memorable to me is what happened next.

We all had to get out of the car and walk to a petrol station and wait for Uncle Norman and his great big V8 Chrysler to come tow us back to his house so they could replace the engine. When Uncle Norman arrived, Dad attached the tiny little gray Morris to the tow line, and situated all his passengers in Uncle Norman's car. Dad then sat himself behind the wheel of the dead little Morris, his face visible to me as I peered through the back window of the powerful Chrysler.

Uncle Norman had to be somewhere that night. At least it seemed that way, because what started out slowly at first gradually got faster and faster. I could see Dad hunkered over the steering wheel gently guiding the little Morris as Uncle Norman started off. After a few minutes Uncle Norman started to accelerate. Dad's face began to turn a pale shade of white. He was fighting the steering on the little car and obviously fighting a losing battle. As the big car got faster, the little car started to slew all over the road. It was like watching the T-birds whip one of their roller skaters around trying to get extra speed. At one point I believe that the little car was up on two wheels. Dad kept mouthing something to me.

Something like "Pullover." I just smiled. "Pullover?" I thought. It was summer and he wouldn't need a pullover this time of year. I waved to him and laughed.

After a particularly long and windy trip, we finally made it safely to Uncle Norman's house. We went back to check on Dad and almost had to pry his white-knuckled hands from the steering column. As you got close to the car, you could actually see smoke coming from the wheel wells and smell the burned brake shoes. I shouldn't have worried about him though; Dad didn't need his pullover because he was really sweating when he got out of the car. In fact, I think he was carsick because he hurled just like I always did.

So what have I learned from this experience?

1. Never assume that your child will only throw up ONCE and then get over it.

2. Never leave a bored child in a complex piece of machinery.

3. Save the roof of your car. Strap your kids down.

4. Never assume that a child will ever understand the word "Stay."

5. Clutch, what's a clutch? I don't need no stinking clutch!

6. The Whip! Not just something you do when water-skiing or while playing Roller Game.

7. Teach your kids to lip read. It might save your life someday.

Life Lesson Number 50

—

"The Double, Triple Dare"

For a few years around the time I was six years old, our family went on holidays to a place called Manly. It is located on the harbor in Sydney and was a very popular holiday resort for the time. We stayed in a small apartment with my parents and grandparents (Mum's parents) and spent our days playing in the sand, sunning ourselves, and swimming in the water.

The swimming area at Manly had a promenade that transversed the beach from a wharf, where the Ferries docked to a rocky point. Under this promenade were bars to stop sharks from getting into the swimming area. It was a beautiful and safe swimming area. However, on top of this promenade was a large diving tower that had two diving levels; the first I had labeled "Stupidly high" and the second, "Death Defyingly High."

As a young boy who could not, swim I was fascinated with the young louts who were jumping off the top of the tower to impress their girlfriends on the beach. My grandfather, Fardie Byrnes, noticed my fascination with it but spent much of his time trying to get me to learn how to swim. I did not want to learn, I wanted to play in the sand.

Fardie realized that I really was not going to try to swim without some enticement, so he "dared me" to learn to swim. Little did he know that I was good at the "dare thing." Dares could go both ways, so I "dared him" to jump off the top of the diving tower. He, of course, refused; after all he was a grandfather. Well, after working our way through the double dares, we finally hit the triple dare stage. I said that I would learn to swim if he would jump off the top "Death Defyingly High" tower. In my adolescent little mind I was safe. There was no way that Fardie would do that. Only crazy people or teenage louts would jump from that height.

He stood there for a moment reflecting on what to do. Then without speaking, he headed off around the wharf and out onto the promenade and up to the top tower of the diving board. I was near panic. He had called my bluff. Would he jump? "No way!" I thought to myself. Stepping forward, he looked down to the water about forty feet below and stepped off into the air.

Mum, Dad and Nana looked on disbelievingly as Fardie hurtled towards the water. It was a lovely jump. Only one problem: Fardie did not keep his legs together. He hit the water with his feet about two feet apart. It seemed like forever before he came back up from under the water. Rather than swimming in immediately he floated for a little while and then slowly side stroked back into the beach where he gingerly made his way up to the towels and sat down. He did not say a word. I knew that he was hurt. The smacking sound as he hit the water had echoed all the way to the beach.

Nana sat behind him trying not to smile. Dad asked if he was all right and Mum wanted to know if she could get him anything. "I don't know why but the back of my neck is killing me!" Fardie said. With that Dad looked at the back of Fardie's neck and there as plain as day you could see two large egg-sized lumps, one on either side of his neck. Dad of course, couldn't let this opportunity go and said, "You've got two big egg-sized lumps on your neck. That will teach you to not close your legs when you hit the water!" Mum and Nana thought that was funny. Fardie did not. After about thirty minutes, Fardie stood up and said, "Come on, it's your turn now!" So we set off down to the waters edge for a lesson in swimming.

We walked out to about chest deep for this little blond-haired boy and Fardie started instructing me on how to do the "Australian Crawl" swimming stroke. It was hard at first and I couldn't get the breathing right, but at least I made forward progress in the water. Fardie said that I could do better than just a few yards at a time, so I took a deep breath, and headed off as fast and hard as I could swimming along the beach. Fardie stood there proudly watching me make headway.

As I finally ran out of breath I figured that it would now be a good time to stop, stand up, and take a breather before setting off again. As I stopped and started to stand up I realized that I had been swimming "out" from the beach rather than "along" the beach. I went down for the first time with my arms flailing as I struggled to get my breath.

When I hit the sand at the bottom I pushed off and burst through the top of the water again to take a breath. After grabbing some quick air and flailing around I sank back under. I went down for the second time. This time I appeared to be out deeper in the water. I struggled back to the surface through sheer effort only to take a breath and go down for the third and last time.

Sitting on the sandy bottom and looking up through the rippling water I can remember thinking, "Where's your grandfather when you really need him?" I was about to die and nobody knew where I was. Just then, two big arms reached down and dragged me back to the surface where I gladly took a deep breath. It was Fardie; he had saved the day again.

I was coughing, spluttering, and crying as he carried me back to the beach. I finally asked him what took so long to save me. He said that he wanted to see if I could swim back into the beach myself. Personally, I think that he was just getting back at me for the two lumps on the back of his neck.

So what have I learned from this experience?

1. Never double, triple-dare a grandfather, because he will call your bluff.

2. Keep your legs together when you jump from great heights.

3. Grandfathers only think they can act like teenagers.

4. Oxygen is a wonderful thing.

5. When you swim along the shore, watch where you're going.

6. Never, ever, ever jump into water from a great height at low tide. You may hit the bottom of the ocean.

7. To this day I can still see the reflected water patterns from my near-drowning day when I close my eyes in bright sunlight.

8. Lumps on the back of your grandfather's neck make him (shall we say) a little testy.

Life Lesson Number 75

—

"A roundabout way of drowning!"

"Well this is a great way to die," I thought to myself. "Drowned in a three inch puddle of water on top of a hill while your Dad is playing cricket. That will look good in the obituary page." I lay face down in a hole filled with muddy water. My chubby little nine-year-old body was trapped in a ridiculous cycle of trying to raise my head out of the water, only to have it whacked back down below the surface at each attempt. This was getting pretty old. Oxygen deprivation was setting in. I needed help and I needed it fast.

That Saturday had started out like any other. Mum, Dad, Steven and I had set out for a picnic at a cricket game in Windsor. We were going to have a family day trip. Dad was going to watch his nephews play, meet a few old friends and reminisce about his own cricketing days. When he got there, his nephews told him that the local team was one man short for the game, so after a short discussion they asked Dad if he would play and he agreed he would.

To an active nine-year-old boy, watching cricket is like sitting still for eight hours of someone dragging his or her fingernails down a chalkboard. It was annoying. I needed a diversion. Dad was off playing cricket. Steven was too young to play with. Oh look, other bored children huddling around a merry-go-round! This might be fun after all. I told Mum that I was going to play in the playground with the other kids. She told me to be careful and to be nice. Nice? I was always nice. I rolled my eyes and set off to play.

I could see why the kids were milling around the merry-go-round. It was a large spinning latticework of pipes that allowed you to sit on it and have someone spin you around. The closer you sat to the middle, the slower you went. The closer to the outside you sat, the faster you went. It had obviously had much use because there was a very deep rut where the kids had dragged their feet over the years. After a few days of recent rain, this rut had filled with muddy and stagnant water.

To a parent, this was a dirty and dangerous trap just waiting to swallow some poor little unsuspecting child. To a nine-year-old boy, this was a challenge. After discussing what we needed to do, we set to seeing how fast we could spin each other and how close we could lower ourselves to the water without actually getting wet. As each of the other kids took their turn, I pushed the merry-go-round faster and faster, all the while goading them to go lower and making fun of them for not being daring enough to lean closer in to the water hazard.

When it came my turn to ride the merry-go-round, I wanted to be sure that these kids did not slack off. I was going to show these kids how it should be done. No one could go faster or hang lower than I could in competitions like this. I instructed them to give it their all when spinning my large frame. If they gave me the speed, I would give them the thrills.

Spinning wildly, I skimmed just above the water, thrilling the masses with my prowess and low-flying technique. It was all fun and games until I lost my grip on the slippery metal. Rather than flying off sideways and out of harm's way, as I should have, I fell through the metal work of the merry-go-round face down into the puddle of water. Given my size, there was only enough clearance in the puddle for my girth to barely clear the swinging bars over my head. Finding myself unable to breathe, I tried to raise my head. I would get it almost out of the water when WHAM, the next spinning bar would knock me face down into the brown slush. Each attempt to raise my head met with the same fate. Wham, wham, wham—this was not looking good. I was getting a headache as well as drowning.

Just as I started to think about what my obituary would read like, some kind cricketer realized that Cliff's little boy was drowning on top of a hill in a three-inch puddle of water. I was rescued. With the merry-go-round stopped, I was raised from the watery grave and led through a phalanx of laughing white-clothed cricketers to the car where my unknowing mother was sitting with Steven. "How embarrassing," I thought to myself. Thank goodness, things couldn't get much worse.

"You can't stay in those wet clothes, Ian, you will catch your death of cold," Mum said. "Come here and take all your clothes off until I dry them," she said. "Oh great," I thought to myself, "now I get to be embarrassed and naked." I was not happy.

For the next three hours I sat naked in the middle of the back seat of Dad's car with a blanket wrapped around me, and outside on a makeshift clothesline, my filthy muddy underwear blowing in the breeze for everyone to see. Every now and then people would walk up to the car window, peer in, and ask if I was the kid who almost drowned on the top of a hill in three inches of water. I just ignored them, pulled the blankets over my head, and hoped that they would go away.

So what have I learned from this experience?

1. When you think things can't get much worse, they will.

2. You can drown in three inches of water.

3. You can drown on top of a hill.

4. I didn't know it then, but this is one of my first "Hey ya'll watch this" moments.

5. Never expect your friends to get you out of trouble when you have just given them a hard time.

6. You will not die if you sit in wet clothes for three hours. Your mother just thinks you will.

7. I find it hard to watch cricket to this day because of flashbacks.

8. The only thing worse than being "the kid that nearly drowned in three inches of water on the top of a hill" is being "the naked kid with his underwear blowing in the breeze that nearly drowned in three inches of water on the top of a hill."

Life Lesson Number 89

—

"Dan, Dan the Dunny Man"

When we first moved to our new home in Blacktown (at that time the outer suburbs of Sydney), we thought that we were in heaven. We had a lovely new home that was all our own. We had a fenced-in yard with a nice driveway for our used (but new to us) Holden car. We had all the amenities that we needed to survive. All, that is, except one.

Each and every house in the new subdivision had a small concrete path leading up the back yard to a small fibro outhouse. What was really special about the outhouse was that it was a one holer without an actual hole. The toilet itself was a metal cover topped off with a wooden toilet seat and lid that could be lifted up to reveal a large tar covered container that contained all the human detritus of the past week. Since we were used to a flush toilet while we lived at Nana's house, this new toilet facility took some getting used to.

This story is not so much about our toilet but about the people who made these toilets work. Both the adults and children of our neighborhood labeled these people "Dunny Men." With no septic system or sewer in town, the local council had come up with a system of picking up the full toilet cans twice a week and replacing them with sterilized fresh empty cans. Needless to say, the job description for this little gem of a job was the butt (no pun intended) of all sorts of jokes around town. Children even had poems about the Dunny Men who emptied their toilets twice each week.

The one poem that I can remember went something like this:

> Dan, Dan the Dunny Man
> Washed his face in a frying pan
> Combed his hair with the leg of a chair
> And told his mother he didn't care

Not too terrible an accusation about poor old Dan, but the fact that we kids were just saying the words Dunny Man caused much laughter and giggling. We always felt sorry for Dan's mother because of her uncaring son.

These Dunny Men actually had it pretty good as far as pay rates were concerned for those years. Let's face it: if I had to come to your house and carry away your excrement twice a week, I would be wanting some sort of premium to do the job. It was at that time one of the best-paid jobs that the local council had. Some of the job perks weren't too bad either. For instance, people left gifts on the toilet seats at Christmas and on other special occasions. These gifts were usually a bottle of beer or some other alcoholic beverage. Given the deplorable conditions that these guys worked under, it couldn't get much better than this (great pay and free beer).

As a Dunny Man, you also had the special working gear that you had to wear. The uniform included a heavy leather apron and shoulder flap, gloves, and great boots with knobby bottoms to keep traction on the slippery ground. I can remember watching these guys work on the odd occasions that I was up early enough to see what went on. Each truck had one driver and two men who worked different sides of the truck as they went from house to house down the street.

Dan would grab an empty can and lid and run up the side of the house to the outhouse out the back. He would lift up the cover, slide out the full can, slide in the empty can, put the cover back on, clamp the lid on the full can and then miraculously hoist the full can up onto his shoulder and run full speed down the side of the house to the truck to repeat the process at the next house. These guys were fighting fit. They were throwing around cans of excrement weighing at least 40 pounds a time for several hundred homes a day.

I can remember thinking that maybe these guys really didn't have it all that bad. Sure they worked under deplorable conditions, but look at the pay they were getting. After all, things really couldn't be that bad, or could they?

One frosty morning I woke to hear the dunny truck pull up in front of our house. I sleepily walked to the lounge room and opened the blinds a crack to see what Dan was up to. The Dan on the other side of the road grabbed his empty can and headed off up the steep driveway of the house across the street. His partner headed off up our driveway to do his dirty work. The Dan from our house made it back to the truck first and tapping the side of the truck indicated to the driver to move on up to the next house.

Now, as best I can tell, this threw off the loading routine somehow, because as the Dan came around into the driveway from the house across the road he realized that the truck had moved thirty yards further up the road. He had to make a critical choice. He could run down the steep and frosty driveway and then head up the road carrying that forty pounds on his shoulders, or he could cut across the frosty yard that sloped down to the front fence, step on the top railing of that three foot fence, jump over and make a beeline to the truck, thus saving himself a little time.

Without even thinking about it, Dan set off across and down the steep slope of the frosty grass, put one foot on the top of the front fence, lifted off, and it was then that his shortcut plan went awry. As he launched himself over the fence, the foot on the top railing slipped off, causing Dan to crash down on his rear end and causing the can to drop and splash its contents like an exploding bomb all over him and all over the yard where he sat. It was a biological nightmare that no twelve-year-old boy needed to see.

I was mesmerized. It was like looking at the horror of a train wreck: you really wanted to look away but couldn't. I just had to see what Dan was going to do.

Dan sat there for a few moments, shaking the fluids from his hands and arms and wiping his face. Without even a comment, he stood up, righted the can, scrapped up all the human detritus with his gloved hands, and prepared to put the lid back on the can. The only thing out of the ordinary was his opposing Dan, who had seen the accident and had stopped to laugh at him before heading off for his next run. The dirty Dan picked up the can, threw it up onto his shoulder, and headed off like nothing had ever happened.

I stood mesmerized thinking to myself that nobody could ever pay me enough to clean up someone else's poop and carry it away. I promised myself that I would never do anything like that and I kept that promise to myself. Well, to tell you the truth, I kept it until we had our first child many years later and I found myself taking care of a particularly messy nappy (diaper). That nappy (diaper) change caused me to have flashbacks to my childhood and visions of Dan, Dan the Dunny Man taking care of our little toilet messes. I realized then what Dan Dan the Dunny Man had figured out many years ago—that good fathers can and will do whatever needs to be done to take care of their families.

So what have I learned from this experience?

1. Whenever I feel bad about my own job, I remember what poor old Dan Dan the Dunny Man had to do.

2. Always wash your hands before you eat. Even if you wear gloves.

3. We need to take more time to appreciate what others do for us.

4. Sometimes it is better not to take the shortcut to our goal.

5. Never say you will never do anything, because invariably you find yourself doing it.

6. These fathers put aside personal pride and did what they needed to do to take care of their families financially.

Life Lesson Number 95

—

"The Porcelain Pony"

I peeked out from under the covers of my bed and held the blankets so that only my eye was visible to anyone in the room. As I looked up at the ceiling I could see the light fitting swinging back and forth in the gloom of the early morning light. I clenched the blanket back closed as a cold clammy sweat came over me and that frightened chill ran up my spine. Was my mind playing tricks on me? Was this some dream turned nightmare? Or was what the preacher had said the night before coming true?

The windowpane next to my bed started to rattle and the light continued to move back and forth. Rousing what courage I could, I uncovered my head and looked at the window and then back at the light. It was confirmed. They were definitely rattling and swinging. This was not good. As I looked out the window again, an eerie golden glow hung over the horizon and pierced the darkness. I sat bolt upright in bed remembering what the preacher had said the night before. All I could think of was his closing phrase, "Like a thief in the night!"

We had a visiting preacher come to our congregation the day before and he had brought a fantastic lesson on "The Day Christ Came Again." In that lesson he had covered all the happenings that would occur when the Lord returned to the earth. To this thirteen-year-old boy with an overactive imagination I had just checked off the first big three: sudden occurrence, earthquake and bright lights. All I needed for confirmation that the world was coming to an end was the sound of trumpets. What was that—was that a horn blowing?

I bounded out of bed and rushed to my parents' room fully expecting them to have been taken up to heaven already. Dad's side of the bed was empty and Mum had assumed the same hiding pose that I had. She had wrapped the blanket over her head and was peeking out with only one eye. I could tell that she was thinking exactly what I was thinking. I said, "Mum, where's Dad. He's gone?" The fear in my voice was evident as I began to believe that both Mum and I had missed the first wave of being taken up to heaven and had obviously been left behind as sinners to take the caboose ride to the lower Hadean realm. She finally mustered enough courage and said, "I don't know where he is."

Well, that's all I needed to confirm that I was in big trouble. The shaking stopped for a few moments and then started again. I had to do something. I had to see if Dad was being taken up in the air, so I ran to the back door, threw it open and stepped out onto the back porch. What I saw only confirmed that this was the big one and that I had been left.

As I stood there I could see that the sides of our above ground pool were flexing in and out with great waves of water flopping up in the middle like a small fountain. The rotary clothesline was rattling from side to side. The dogs and animals of the area were going absolutely crazy and the golden rays of light were breaking through the dark clouds and were making angelic rays shoot from their source.

As I looked up into the brightening rays I cried out my question in despair, "Daddy?"

"What?" came the answer from only a few feet away.

This shocked me, as I was looking skyward thinking that he had made "the big trip." I looked again at the pool and the clothesline and listened to the barking dogs and looked at the shining light. I then realized that the response to my question had come from the laundry room that ran off to the left of our back porch. It was in here that we had placed our new flush toilet.

I slowly opened the door to see my Dad sitting on "the Perch" as we called it. His trousers were around his ankles, his newspaper had dropped to the floor in front of him, and he was holding on to either side of the toilet lid with both hands as it appeared to sway with the same motion as the pool.

"What's happening, Dad?" I asked hesitantly, expecting him to confirm my end-of-days analysis.

"Earthquake, Son," was his only response as he held on for dear life.

What a relief that was to a young boy who thought he had been left behind!

"OK," I said as I closed the door and stepped back inside the house.

Radio and television later that morning reported an earthquake in Sydney that was quite large for this area of the country. They reported several large aftershocks as well. The reports concluded that there had been no apparent damage or injury caused by these earthquakes. What they didn't know was that there had been damage and injury at our house.

In the process of riding out the quake on our new porcelain pony, Dad had broken the toilet seat, and had pinched his rear end quite terribly. Thank goodness he had not been thrown from his trusty steed. I guess all that horse breaking when he was young had finally paid off.

So what have I learned from this experience?

1. Active imaginations can run away from you given a few small facts.

2. Preachers can paint images that will stay with you for a lifetime.

3. You should always question whether you're ready to make the big trip at any time.

4. Car horns can be misinterpreted as trumpets.

5. A beautiful sunrise and an earthquake do not make for the second coming.

6. Learn to ride horses early in life and it might save your life later.

7. When buying toilet seats, don't get the flimsy cheap ones. Go for something a little sturdier.

8. Only a true friend will put Band-Aids on your injured bottom.

Life Lesson Number 140

—

"Dad's Discipline—The Leather"

Discipline at the Shepherd home was always fair, swift, and just. Susan, Steven and I all knew what it meant when Dad said that we needed "a bit of a touch up with the leather." When we were younger we knew we were in trouble if he said that phrase and then started to undo his belt. At least then I had the common sense to stand still while he gave us a much needed whack with the old leather belt, spoke to us about what we had done wrong, and then allowed us to go penitently on our way.

Something about this discipline process changed when I was about ten years old. I don't know what came over me, but at that age I started to reason in my prepubescent mind that I could outrun my father. He was, after all in his thirties now (quite near death from a ten-year-old's perspective), and that made him a real old man. Besides, there was no way that he could keep up with a young whippersnapper like me. Of course, I gave no thought at all to what I would do if I did actually manage to escape the wrath of Cliff. I had no plan after having made my break for freedom. If worse came to worse, I could always live in the shed or sleep under the house or I could always go and live with my Aunty and Uncle who lived next door. They would take me in.

I can't remember what I did that caused me to be standing there about to get the leather that day. I knew that Dad was not happy. He had used the phrase "a bit of a touch up with the leather" at least twice and was in the process of undoing his belt. Our eyes were locked on each other and I was frozen like a kangaroo in a spotlight. I was mesmerized by the slow motion scene that was unfolding. It was then that Dad's belt caught in one of his belt loops as he tried to whip it out with his normal flourish. When this happened he broke eye contact with me as he fumbled with the belt. That broke the spell. This was my chance to make a hasty getaway.

A look of dismay came over Dad's face as he realized what was happening. This was an unusual occurrence. I think he took some amusement in the fact that I was now adding a little sport to this sometimes-tiresome event. I shot off to Dad's left, because he couldn't get the belt off and swing to hit me that way. I had one chance at making this a successful escape and, of course, in a moment of sheer panic, I made the wrong choice. I could have turned right and gone out the front door. I could have turned left and headed out the back door, but no, I set off up the dead end hallway, ending up in my bedroom with no means of escape. I had just jumped from the frying pan and landed in the fire.

When I got into the bedroom, I realized my mistake. There were too many toys under my bed and I was too "rotund" to secret myself away there. I had the same problem with my closet. It too was full of the detritus of childhood and there was no room for a wayward son. I stood there for what seemed like forever waiting for the stampeding father to round the corner and give me the father of all beltings with the leather. I waited and waited, but no Dad. Then I heard him ambling up the creaky hallway.

Parents may be old but they are not stupid. He knew that he had me like a rabbit in a trap and I think he stopped to enjoy the stupidity of what I had just done. After a few moments his large frame appeared at the door. As he stood at the door looking at me, I could see that he had to wipe a quick smile off his face. I guess he saw in me the horror and recognition of the stupid mistake that I had just made. In my mind, nothing could save me now, or could it?

I don't know what possessed me to do what I did next. I had never considered it before but would always consider it an option later in my young troublemaking life. As Dad whipped out the belt (this time with no problem), I broke for the bedroom window, threw it open, stuck my head out, and started screaming, "Someone get the Police! Someone get the Police!" After the first two rounds of yelling, I got the first whack from the belt over my behind, which was so conveniently stuck out, presenting an easy target for Dad. With each whack of the belt, I yelled louder.

After I had received five whacks with the belt, our neighbor, Aunty Peg, came running around the side of her house to see what was going on. I had not noticed that Dad had stopped whacking my behind and that he was holding his stomach laughing. I just continued to yell. Aunty Peg rushed over to the fence and asked what was going on. Dad leaned over and looked out the window laughing and told her that I was "getting the leather." At that point, she burst into laughter and said, "Well, good for you Cliff! Let him have another!"

I thought that I was done for, but then I noticed that they were both laughing uncontrollably, the belting forgotten. I realized that I had done it. I had saved myself by my bizarre and unusual ten-year-old tactics. I filed this little episode away for future use.

So what have I learned from this experience?

1. A father should never break eye contact with his child during the discipline process.

2. If you must run, have an escape plan! You can't think straight when it's all "elbows and knees" to get out of the way.

3. Clean out your closet and underneath your bed regularly. You never know when you might need to hide there.

4. Remember that if you run, you eventually have to come home.

5. Age, belt skills, and patience will overcome youth, stupidity, and speed any day.

6. Don't rely on your neighbors to side with you. They take the side of the parent every time.

7. This is the only belting with Dad's strap that I can remember. I know I had others, but I can't even remember them.

Life Lesson Number 143

—

"The Wrath of Mum!"

You would think that a ten-year-old boy would learn from his experiences. If you did, you were only half right. The last time I got "a bit of a touchup with the leather" from my father I had successfully diverted a good spanking. How did that happen? In the mind of a ten-year-old boy, that happened because "I ran away." It never did strike me that the resulting situation was funny and that this had diverted my father from his paternal task of correcting his blonde-headed boy.

I had stored away this little escape scenario in the back of my mind for several weeks. If it worked once, it might work again. Little did I know how right I might be and how soon I would find out.

Each year my mother would help prepare crafts and gifts for the school fete (school festival). One of her craft specialties that we all could work on together as a family was a Kewpie Doll (a small doll dressed in a ballerina tutu tied to a small walking cane made from bamboo). We had a great time working on putting these crafts together. Mother would sew the tutu, I would put it on the doll, Steven would attach the doll to the Kewpie Doll cane and Susan would stack them up for us.

At the end of one of these craft sessions, Dad noticed that we had one Kewpie Doll stick left over. He jokingly said that it would make a great emergency replacement for the leather and then put that stick up over the kitchen door where it could be retrieved at a moment's notice to settle any discipline issues that might arise.

Steven, Sue and I looked at each other. Now we had the leather and the stick. The world was so unfair.

Once again, I cannot remember what I did that night in the kitchen that required the hasty retrieval of the stick. I do remember that Dad did not have on his trusty belt (and that was a good thing!). I think Dad broke eye contact with me purposefully that night to see if I would run. Remembering that I had been successful in my last escape attempt, I decided to break cover and run just one more time. This time I started using the kitchen table and chairs for cover as Dad took several swipes at my legs. The fact that he was swatting and not hitting must have been frustrating because he doubled his efforts to catch me as we circled the kitchen table.

Since I had been in chase mode once before and had suffered with a bad choice of exits, you would think that a young boy would learn and make for the closest outside exit. If you thought that, you are again wrong. The "duffus factor" had set in yet again and I decided to make the turn out of the kitchen and head back up the hall to my bedroom. All the while Dad was gaining on me.

As Dad reared back to take one final mighty swing at the back of my legs I turned the corner to leave the kitchen. Through some miraculous alignment of cosmic events, my mother stepped around the door, her arms filled with a basket of folded washing. The arrival of both her shins at the exact spot where my chubby calves had been at the exact moment that Dad had swung was a sight to behold.

The Kewpie Doll stick whacked both her shins so hard that she stopped in her tracks. Blood flowed to her head and face so that she looked like a Roman Candle about to burst. I stopped dead in my tracks and stared. Dad stood up, his face white as a ghost, with the cane in his hand and a look of total horror on his face. Then the strangest thing happened. Mum said absolutely nothing. She just stood there as we waited for the volcano to explode. Then, slowly she bent down, placed the clothesbasket on the floor and stood back erect. Without a word, she reached out to my father, snatched the Kewpie Doll stick from his hands, and meticulously broke it into pieces three inches long. When her task was complete, she handed the pieces back to Dad, picked up her washing basket and walked outside.

What a relief that was! The cut and run strategy had worked again from the point of view of a ten-year-old. However, from the father's perspective, the thrill of the chase had been replaced by the father's urge for "self-preservation." We never saw another Kewpie Doll stick in our house.

So what have I learned from this experience?

1. Timing is everything.

2. Never assume that you know what is around the next corner.

3. Always wear a belt.

4. What Mother didn't say and what she did gave us years of stories at the dinner table.

5. Actions speak louder than words.

6. Fathers should never break eye contact with their children during the discipline process, even in jest.

7. A father and son can bond over the strangest things in their lives.

Life Lesson Number 145

—

"Brothers and Sisters and Bears, Oh My!"

Do you know what happens to bored five-year-old boys? That's right. They grow up to be bored eleven-year-old boys. One would think that with age a bored eleven-year-old boy would change his habits. If you did, you were wrong. The bored eleven-year-old doesn't change his habits he just changes his toys.

It didn't take long for my parents to figure out that cats and I "just didn't get along." Something about the poor little cat's karma must have told them that to spare the species they needed to move on to some other form of diversion for their golden haired boy. Thankfully they did.

When we picked up my brother from the hospital after he was born, my mother and father looked at him and said, "Isn't he wonderful, Ian!" I just looked at him and said to myself, "Oh goody, a new toy!" Sadly, when my parents, brother and I picked up our new baby sister after she was born, we went through the same ritual, only my statement changed to "Oh goody, two toys!" Unfortunately, I would have to wait a few years for them to be any good to play with. That would give me some time to make up some new "games."

When I was eleven-years-old, my brother Steven was about to be five-years-old, and my sister Susan was about to be two and a half years old. Things were starting to get interesting around the Shepherd household. I had yet to see any of the brilliant logic that I had exhibited as a child in my brother. He was, for all-intents and purposes, pretty boring to me. He didn't get into trouble, he didn't throw tantrums, and he had never swung a cat from the clothesline. Susan was much the same. She toddled around the house with her little bowl cut hairdo and was basically just cute. How boring!

I had noticed that both Steven and Susan had formed attachments to two stuffed animals as they were growing up. Susan had latched onto a small four-inch tall koala bear and she had named him "Billy" the bear. Billy went everywhere with Susan and she could not spend more than a few minutes away from him without wondering where he was. She had loved that little bear so much that the fur had started to wear off him. After several failed attempts to replace the real "Billy the Bear" with a new "Billy the Bear," Mum finally gave up and made a little red coat for Billy to wear to hide his bald spots.

Steven felt the same way about his "Squirrel." Squirrel was a cloth imprint of a bushy tailed squirrel that you sewed together, filled with chopped up foam, and then sewed the bottom shut. Squirrel was about twelve inches high and had a small foot that poked out at the bottom. Steven couldn't go to sleep without cuddling squirrel and rubbing his soft little foot on his hand (much the same as other children do with their security blankets). Although he was only a cheap toy that Mum had made to sell at the school fete (school festival), he was the most loved toy that Steven ever had.

As luck would have it, I had finally realized that I got the leather whenever "I" did anything wrong. This realization caused the mind of this eleven-year-old to go into overtime trying to find a solution to this boredom and keep myself out of trouble. "What if," I said to myself, "I wasn't the one that appeared to be causing the trouble? Why get into trouble yourself, if you can have others do it for you!" I had the toys; now all I needed was a plan.

Having been a five-year-old myself, I knew how the power of suggestion could plant ideas into the complex thinking patterns of these children. I set out to instigate what would become a running battle between my brother and sister. Why fight a war yourself when you can get others to do it for you? I would be the Jedi Master using my mind games over these young ones.

It all started simply with a suggestion, like "Steven, why don't you hide Billy from Susan for a while!" and "Susan, why don't you take Squirrel and put him under your bed!" Of course, they did exactly as they were told. The tearful scenes that followed were quite amusing, not only because of the mayhem that ensued, but because the child that actually hid the toys got into trouble, not me. This was great, but after a few weeks of this I felt that I needed to step it up a notch.

I decided that just hiding Billy and Squirrel was too amateurish. So "things" started happening to Billy and Squirrel. I would tell Steven to remove Billy's clothes and hide them, or run into the room, grab Billy from Susan, punch the small koala in the face five times, drop him and run back out. Susan, on the other hand, might take Squirrel and put him in the bathtub, thus soaking him. The mental anguish that Steven went through as Squirrel hung pegged out to dry on the clothesline was terrible. All the while the focus was on the two smaller children while I sat quietly watching the mayhem that ensued.

Eventually, Steven started to catch on that he was the one that got into trouble all the time and that I was left alone. This was a new wrinkle in the mind game of life, but one that could be overcome. I decided to step this game up yet another level, and I started taking Squirrel hostage until Steven had perpetrated some heinous crime on poor little Billy the bear.

The final straw for my parents was the day that I set up the double-double cross. I had both Susan and Steven working against each other. This took some doing and required me to threaten my dear little brother. How did I threaten him? I had put a very tight elastic band around the foot of his squirrel (the foot that he rubbed on his hand to go to sleep each night) and told him that the blood had been cut off too long and that the foot was going to fall off. It could probably be saved but only if he would get Billy one last time. He agreed. Kids are so easy to manipulate.

While Susan was distracted, Steven retrieved Billy and brought him into the living room. We fashioned a small hangman's noose out of the Venetian blind cord, carefully raised the blinds, tied the noose around Billy's neck and sat the bear down on the chair ready for a lynching. Of course, while all this was going on, Susan had been instructed to take Squirrel and carefully put clothes pegs all over him in the bedroom. He looked like a porcupine and quite obviously would have been in severe Squirrel pain.

With the setup complete I took it upon myself to casually ask my sister, "Where's Billy?" She, of course, set off on a rampage through the house trying to find Billy. At the moment that she stepped into the living room, Steven said, "Here he is!", pointed to the koala, and pulled on the Venetian cord. This caused the blinds to drop, and Billy the bear to shoot up and hang by the neck until dead. The screams from Susan were inconsolable as her lovely bear hung obviously near death. My work here was almost done. "Where's Squirrel?" I said to no one in particular.

With that Steven set off on his own quest through the house howling about how people kept taking and hurting his squirrel. When he found Squirrel "pegged to death," things started to fall apart. The two children took to each other with a relish. With all the wailing, Billy-thumping, accusing, Squirrel-whacking, and howling my parents finally got involved, debriefed the young tormentees and settled on who was the real culprit.

I did not run from the leather that day; I had learned that much in my eleven years. My life as a Jedi mind master may have been over, but at least I still had my two toys play with.

So what have I learned from this experience?

1.   The Military should probably study the minds of bored eleven-year-olds to improve their own Psychological Operations programs.

2.   Nighttime Billy kidnapping raids can be fun for half the family.

3.   You can stuff a foam-filled cloth Squirrel into your father's shoe and people won't find it for days.

4.   Five-year-olds do not comprehend the circulatory system of a foam Squirrel's foot.

5.   You can try to shave a "Billy the koala," but his fur won't grow back.

6.   From a five-year-old's perspective, you can be "pegged to death."

Life Lesson Number 155

—

"What's in a name?"

Growing up as a young Aussie, you faced many challenges. Usually the first challenge was what your friends would call you when you went to school. Anywhere else in the world this might not have been a traumatic event, but in Australia once you were labeled with a nickname you were stuck with that name for life. Well, if not for life, then at least until a better name came along, so you always hoped that you would get a good nickname when you first came in the kindergarten gate.

Australians have a knack for using word games called "rhyming slang." Rather than saying "he is my mate," an Aussie would say, "he's my china plate;" china plate rhymes with mate, thus the slang usage. Any Aussie understands this rhyming game, but it often throws foreigners off in conversations. When it comes to nicknames, which Aussies prefer to use rather than real names, the selection process is often long, arduous and cruel. It involves an analysis of both physical and mental states and careful consideration of the way one's name or surname might be spelled. Rhyming slang often played a part in the name that you were given.

If you were lucky, you had an obvious trait that automatically had a name assigned to it. For instance, if you had red hair, you were automatically called Blue. Why? I don't know, and it doesn't really matter. You were just called Blue, because thousands of other red heads had been given that name. If you were tall you were sure to be called either Stumpy (note the opposite inference here) or Lofty. If you were tall and somewhat skinny, you were guaranteed to be called Stalk, because of your bird like qualities.

Particular attention was always given to the most noticeable and probably the worst trait that you had. If you were fat, you were called either Tiny or Skinny. If you looked sickly, you might be called Spew. If you were ugly, you were called Face. Things were tougher if you were not originally from Australia. If you were of Asian origin, you probably were called China; or if you had dark skin, you might have been called Mid-Night. During the early 60's, these were all taken in good jest, as your best friends were the ones doing the naming. Today, the politically correct crowd would have a heart attack at how people named each other.

If you were not one of the lucky few that were easily named by an attribute, you fell into the next method of naming. This usually relied on the addition of certain letters to your name. In most cases the persons being named had a "Y" or an "O" or an "A" added to the end of their name; for instance, Steve would become Stevo, Bob would become Bobby, Don would become Donny, and Barry would become Bazza. I think you see what I am getting at here. Sometimes the "Y" or "O" or "A" might be added to a shortened last name; for instance Shepherd became Shepo or Simmons became Simmo, and McKenzie became Maca, all quite confusing to the unknowing outsider.

If you fell through the naming cracks to this point, one of the last resorts was to add an "er" to the name; for instance, if your last name was Klingenberg, it was shortened and had an "er added to it to become Klinger. It was all quite logical, at least to the young Aussie.

If adding the "er" didn't work for you, then you were doomed. You were called by your regular name until such time as you did something stupid or something became known about you. These kids lived in fear awaiting their most embarrassing experience. Heaven help it if you had fallen to this naming stage and broke wind in class. You were labeled Thunder Bum from that day on.

Of course, it was not uncommon for your nickname to change if some new fact came out that was just too good to ignore. For instance, Cliffy (my Dad Clifton) became the Pea Patch Kid when he was in the army. He was labeled that because of his weekend furloughs to work on the farm.

When one of our friends managed to get electrocuted, he was henceforth and forevermore know as Sparky. Another was renamed Fish after a particularly bad bladder infection and some disquieting bladder accidents that rendered him waterlogged in the classroom. Cold, yes, but generally accepted by the male population as a rite of passage.

I actually managed to make it through to high school as Shepo. Thank goodness, I had avoided the name Iany. That nomdeplume would have been a fate worse than death for a chubby kid. Rhyming slang wise it bordered on Tiny, which was the equivalent of being called Fatso. I lost the nickname Shepo when the appearance of my brother at the same school forced a name change on me. I went from Shepo to Big Shep. Steven, my brother, became Little Shep. I know, it doesn't quite fit the naming convention mentioned above, but at least it wasn't cruel and demeaning.

During my rugby days I fought off a new nickname that the boys tried to give me. For several weeks the team had noticed that when I ran, my legs turned bright red. Thus they tried to pin the nickname Lobster on me. It was a tough fight, but I managed to end up as Big Shep after a few heated arguments.

So being an older Aussie now, what do I have to look forward to? Well, if I go bald I can be sure that my closest Aussie friends will change my nickname to Curly or Nude Nut. If I lose a limb or digit, I will be labeled Nub or Stump. If I grow a beard, I will be called Fungus Face. If various internal organs start to shut down, I will be called Bung. One can only hope that when things start falling off that they are clearly visible. Heaven help me if my friends ever find out about my serious hemorrhoid condition; I couldn't face the rest of my life being called "Farmer Giles."

So what have I learned from this experience?

1. If your child has a runny nose the first day of kindergarten, don't send the poor little kid to school. He will forever be known as Booger or Candles.

2. If your child has a gas problem, treat it medically. He could go through life being called Blurt, Stinker, Pong or Thunder Bum.

3. If your child is prone to throwing up in stressful situations, be prepared to call him Ruth, Ralph or Chuck Chunder for the rest of his life.

4. Parents, run through the rhyming name game before you slap down a name on a poor unsuspecting little child. You would be amazed at what horrid things rhyme with your child's name.

5. If teeth need fixing, go ahead and get them done early. It's hard to throw names like Bucky and Fang once they have been attached.

6. For those of you who are rhyming slang impaired: hemorrhoids are piles; piles rhymes with Farmer Giles.

7. If your name is Mark, that's close to Markus, which rhymes with Farcus, which when combined becomes Markus Farcus (a good name for any brother-in-law). Can you see how much fun this is?

8. The next time someone says, "What's in a name?" Punch him. He obviously never grew up in Australia.

Life Lesson Number 165

—

"The Conscientious Objector"

In the 50's when Dad was a young fellow growing up on the farm, Australia had national service. Each young man was required to do a certain amount of time in the Australian Army in preparation for any war that might come about. Dad spent a lot of time thinking about this stint in the army, and like many young Christians of that time, he found it hard to reconcile taking a life in battle with the principles that he believed in. He figured that if it came down to taking a life that he could not do it.

When it came time to sign up for the army Dad and his cousin Dennis both applied for conscientious objector status. They had to go to court and defend their beliefs in front of the judge, which they did. Dad and Dennis told wild stories about how they had to argue from the Bible about their beliefs, finally causing the judge to rule in their favor. What happened to them though was not unusual. They won the right not to fight, but they were given the status of non-combatants in the medical core.

When you think about that for a minute, it is quite funny. They were training to go into the hottest fighting areas, under heavy fire, and all the while carrying only a medical pack. They were tasked with dragging out mortally wounded men under fire. Sounds to me that the government got what it wanted and Dad and Dennis got what they wanted. It appeared to be a win-win situation.

When we were clearing out Dad's closet after he passed away, we found the court order documents stating that Dad was granted the status of conscientious objector based on religious belief. We filed it away carefully, so that we could keep it for posterity, but the wording of "non-combatant" didn't really ring true for my Dad. Obviously Dad was not a coward as many people tried to label these conscientious objectors. Dad trained as hard as anyone else and by taking the medical assignment had agreed to go under fire without the chance to defend himself if need be. This to me was a choice that showed that my Dad was not afraid of bit of a "barney" (fight) if one came his way.

We had always given him a hard time about his time in the National Service joking about how he would never fight if the need arose. We used to joke about what he would do if any of us got into trouble and he had to defend us. Our stories always ended up with us all running away. Dad would just sit and smile back at us with a knowing look that told us a different story. Underneath that gentle giant exterior was a fiercely protective father that we did not see.

Our opinion of Dad changed one day when he told us the story of a "small problem" that he had on the way home from work that day. Dad had been changing lanes trying to get a better position and had accidentally cut off another gentleman and his wife in their car. Dad said that he had done the wrong thing and admitted that it was his mistake. He indicated to the other driver that he was sorry and continued on his way remorseful.

Apparently the driver in the car that Dad had cut off had different ideas. He started to swerve around Dad and abuse him. Dad just put his foot down and accelerated away trying to leave the other driver behind. This was not to be so.

At the next red traffic light Dad had to stop behind a car in the right lane right next to the center island of the road (remember that they drive on the left side of the road in Australia). Having stopped, he looked into the rear vision mirror to see the angry driver and his wife careening up behind his blocked-in car. Dad watched in the rear vision mirror as the gentleman stepped out of his car, started rolling up his sleeves and began to verbally threaten Dad's life as he walked towards Dad's open driver side window.

Dad said that he had two choices: he could sit still and let the gentleman beat him or the car to pieces or he could step out of the car and talk the man down. With the traffic light still red, he stepped out of the car and stood facing the angry driver. As the driver stepped towards Dad he appeared to be preparing to rear back and punch Dad. Dad said he didn't even think about it: before the other driver could finish winding up, Dad dropped him in the middle of the highway with a single punch to the chin. The driver was out cold on the road. Dad guessed talking would do no good now.

Dad didn't know what to do next. He thought for a moment, bent over, picked up the unconscious driver, dragged him safely to the center island of the highway, positioned him carefully so as not to choke, waved to the lady in the car and left. As Dad drove off, he looked in the rear vision mirror to see the wife sitting bug-eyed with her mouth open in the car.

We never again gave Dad a hard time again about being a non-combatant after this little incident. We also marveled at the stupidity of anyone who might get on the wrong side of that quiet conscientious objector from the bush.

So what have I learned from this experience?

1. Bravery and beliefs are not mutually exclusive.

2. Given a choice of fight or flight, Cliffy chose fight and flight. Unusual, but effective.

3. Be careful of the quiet ones; their reactions might surprise you.

4. After this Dad always said, "If you have to hit, there should only be two hits. You hitting him and him hitting the pavement."

5. This story made Dad a legend in his kids' minds.

6. The next time someone on the highway cuts you off and you want to react, just imagine waking up on a median strip with a very sore jaw, an aggravated wife, and lots of snarled traffic behind your car. You might just change your mind!

Life Lesson Number 175

—

"The Pits"

Church camp was always held the week between Christmas and New Year's day. It was the one big event that we teenagers looked forward to all year and all the small churches in Sydney tried to attend the camp. It was a great place to renew old friendships, meet new people, and, for the teenage boys amongst the campers, get into trouble.

The campsite itself was located in the mountains at Kurrajong Heights about forty miles from Sydney. It was a fairly primitive camp location with a closed in kitchen, covered eating area and a few cabins that would barely hold the small number of teenage girls who were brave enough to come to camp.

The boys being rougher and tougher than the females got to sleep in army tents or in their own tent accommodation at the other end of the campsite. When I say it was a primitive location, I really mean primitive. There was no city water, so any water that you used came from storage tanks that were filled during the rainy season. If they ran empty during camp, you paid to have water hauled up to the camp by the fire department. Each and every glass of water that you drank from these tanks had mosquito "wigglies" in it. There was nothing like getting your protein and liquids at the same time.

The toilets for the boys were most interesting. They were located at the bottom of the hill right near where the tents were located. These were not your usual toilets. They were what you might call a "ten holer" with ten separate toilet stalls located over a very large pit. Each cubicle had a wooden bench and a wooden lid that covered the hole and kept in the stench from down below. All these lovely stalls were surrounded by corrugated iron, which stored the heat and provided perfect shelter for the deadly spider population of the bush. You were taking your life in your hands if you spent too much time in the pit toilets.

Since Australia is in the southern hemisphere, the week of camp was usually tremendously hot, especially for those of us who were lucky enough to be sleeping in tents. It was during these hot and sleepless nights that the wicked minds of the teenage boy campers were their most active. Schemes were formed, tricks were planned, and unapproved night excursions were put into operation. Our small band of wayward brothers was not unlike the crew from Hogan's Heroes. From our perspective we were being held captive in a church camp with very strict rules that either needed to be stretched or slightly broken. We always tried to push the envelope as far as we could. We never did any harm to property and we never really meant to harm anyone physically. Of course, our poor victim's mental state was always up for grabs.

The camp director and his counselors, on the other hand, tried to curtail any special nocturnal activities that the malfeasant few tried to put together. It was at best a battle of wits to see who could outmaneuver the other. The camp leaders relied heavily on insider information to find out what was going to happen to whom and when any said incursions might be made. They had been getting good information on our sorties. There was a stoolpigeon amongst us. We knew it and it didn't take us long to figure out who it was.

On this one particularly hot and sticky night, Greg Klingenberg and I had decided that we were going to get Mark Farrell. Why Farrell? Because he had tried to wrangle his way into our double secret hideout in the bush called "Pikers Corner." Pikers Corner was a small clearing where the select lazy few had set up hammocks, chairs and coolers so that we could hide from Colonel Klink (the camp director) and his henchmen. "They couldn't make you work if they couldn't find you" was our theory. Farrell, not a member of the select lazy few, had other ideas of his own. If he couldn't stay with us in our secret area, then he would dob (rat) us all in and tell them where the hideout was and what we got up to while we were there. There was no doubt about it. Farrell had to go. He was the annoying little brother that everyone wanted to tie up in a tree and forget.

That night Klingenberg and I had been closely monitoring Farrell's tent for any movement. Our patience paid off at about 11:10 pm when Farrell unzipped his pup tent and made a beeline for the Pits. This was our chance. He had separated himself from the herd. It was late at night and no one else appeared to be in the Pits. This was perfect, we could sneak up on Farrell, kick in the dunny door to his cubicle, grab him and give him the equivalent of a swirly with his head down the pit hole. It was a fate so horrid that even I almost retched at the thought, and yet it fit the crime. That would teach him to even consider dobbing us in to Colonel Klink the camp director.

We watched Farrell enter the pits and gave him a few moments to become suitably indisposed. Watching out for the Colonels henchmen, we cautiously made our way down to the door of the pits, slid inside quietly, and began checking under the stalls for Farrell feet. Yep, only one pair of shoes in this building and they had to be Farrell's. He was the only one that went into the building prior to the raid. The dim lighting was going to be a bit of a problem. Thank goodness, Klingenberg had his flashlight ready to illuminate the culprit as we entered the stall. We wanted to see the stark horror on his face as he realized he was going to pay for his treachery with the stinkiest swirly of his life.

Stepping back and standing side by side like Starsky and Hutch on a bust, we prepared to kick in the dunny door and grab our man. With one massive kick the door crashed open and the flashlight shone onto a newspaper being held close to someone's face. It was dim in the stall, but you could read if you held materials close to your face. "Funny," I thought to myself, "I don't remember Farrell carrying a newspaper with him." As we stood there dumbfounded, the newspaper slowly lowered to reveal Colonel Klink, our camp director, sitting on the throne in all his glory.

I was absolutely horrified. My reputation was ruined. I looked at Klingenberg. Klingenberg looked at me. We both looked at Colonel Klink sitting on the toilet. Not a word had been spoken. Now, I don't know what possessed Klingenberg to do it, but as best I could tell it was Klingenberg's feeble attempt to grasp some reasonable explanation for busting in on the director of the camp while he sat on the toilet. Klingenberg's singing suddenly broke the silence. The words came softly at first but then with a little more gusto—

Happy birthday to you,
happy birthday to you,
happy birthday dear director,
happy birthday to you!

It was pure genius. Ridiculous, yes, but still pure genius!

Colonel Klink rolled his eyes, and lifting his newspaper closer to his face, began to read again. He never uttered a word or mentioned that incident to us again. That slippery little Farrell on the other hand would still have to pay for his indiscretions. We never did figure out how he got out of the pits without us seeing him.

So what have I learned from this experience?

1. You can't judge a cubicle by its shoes.

2. Never assume that what you saw go into the toilet is what is actually sitting there.

3. The Farrell clan is apparently immune to large doses of Epsom Salts (Exlax).

4. Bowels and bladders must be infinitely expandable because Farrell didn't go to the bathroom for the remaining three days of camp.

5. Quick and effective random abstract thinking is hard to come by in stressful situations.

6. You should never attempt to give the camp director a swirly. He could turn out to be your father-in-law one day.

Life Lesson Number 199

—

"The Poor Little Pus-Eyed Kitten"

.

We had just returned from America after our wedding there and had just been re-married for my family in Australia. One might think that two weddings would be great. If you did, you were right. The second wedding was much more fun and a lot more relaxed than the first. But two honeymoons? Maybe that's not such a great idea.

After our second wedding in Sydney, we had arranged to take a long weekend at the old holiday home rental at Ettalong. Each year as a child I had spent a month in this old house with our extended family fishing, playing in the sand, and canoeing in the ocean. The place brought back fond memories for me and I thought that this would be a good time to get my new bride into the swing of things by taking her there to show her "how special" the place really was.

As I walked into the rental office, old Mrs. Anderson greeted me, and several large cats and about eight small kittens surrounded her. As I signed in and took the key from her, I noticed that one of the kittens' eyes were swollen shut with pus running from them. I should have turned and said nothing, but, of course, I didn't. I asked her what was wrong with the kitten. To an old widow lady that was an open invitation to get the entire cat genealogy of who was whose kitten and how old each cat was and let's not forget to mention all their names as well. Finally, after several minutes of feline introductions, she came down to the poor little pus-eyed kitten and its sad situation.

It turns out that this poor little pus-eyed kitten had been sick for weeks and regardless of how often she had asked her grown sons to come and take the poor little pus-eyed kitten to be put down they had refused. They were too soft hearted. I smiled at myself. After all, I had a special relationship with cats. Well, to cut a long story short, she offered to take off a few dollars in rent if I would "take care of" the poor little pus-eyed kitten. "No worries!" I said as I paid the lower rent, picked up the poor little pus-eyed kitten and walked out the door.

Mrs. Anderson's house backed onto a boatshed and dock that extended a long way out into the bay. As I walked down the steps, I noticed an old Hessian (Burlap) bag and some loose house bricks under the side of the house. Without thinking, I picked up the Hessian bag, dropped in the brick, dropped in the poor little pus-eyed kitten and, tying the top shut, headed off down the driveway past my wife (who was sitting in the car waiting for the key) and out onto the wharf. When I reached the end of the wharf, I took three turns around my head with the Hessian bag and lobbed it out into the briny blue. I turned and headed back in to unload the car.

I had only been married a few days. I don't know what I was thinking. Perhaps in hindsight I should have kept the poor little pus-eyed kitten death squad incident a secret known only to myself, to Mrs. Anderson and to the poor little pus-eyed kitten. But no, I proudly march up to my new wife and blurt out, "You know how much money I just saved?" Not even thinking that she would ask, "And how did you get her to cut down on the cost of the rent?" When this little gem of a question hit me, I realized that I was in trouble. After stammering around for a plausible answer, I finally looked at her, dropped my shoulders, and blurted out the truth. "She paid me to put her poor little pus-eyed kitten in a bag with a house brick and throw it off the end of the wharf!" (Well, it was almost all the truth.)

The look of stark horror on my new wife's face was amazing. I could see what she was thinking: "I have just married a poor little pus-eyed kitten-murdering monster capable of disposing of dead bodies without a second thought!" Tears filled her eyes and she stormed into the house. This was going well, wasn't it?

Needless to say, the rest of my weekend didn't get any better. I tried everything, but every conversation somehow turned to that poor little pus-eyed kitten floating on the ocean floor in a bag with a house brick. I gave in; I could not win anyway that I tried.

Now, remember that I had only been married a few days and I was still "thinking single." The single guy in me said, "Try the humor route. That will work!" So every time she brought up that stupid poor little pus-eyed kitten thing, I started to mimic a poor little pus-eyed kitten holding its breath in a Hessian bag waiting to be rescued. I thought it was cute as I rolled out lines like, "I sure hope they get out here soon! I can't hold my breath much longer!" or "Do you think they might throw me a can of Nine Lives; I'm starting to get hungry?" Each classic line was greeted with an icy stare that should have caused fear in any normal married man. I was no normal man. I was a marital neophyte when it came to understanding women and I was way out of my depth.

Finally, it struck me that the only way out of this was to admit what I had done. So I did what any married man would do, I walked right up to her, looked her in the eye and lied to save my own bacon.

"Honey," I said, "you're right! I'm so sorry! I shouldn't have listened to that horrible old widow lady and drowned her poor little pus-eyed kitten in such a horrible and grotesque fashion. I don't know what came over me! Please forgive me?" Tears filled her eyes, as she looked lovingly at me, a broken and contrite man. Things were going to get better.

So what have I learned from this experience?

1. The "Vinny Barbarino" defense of "What? Where? And When?" doesn't work if your wife sees you toss the poor little pus-eyed kitten bag in the water.

2. If you break down under cross-examination, at least give some semblance of the truth as your explanation.

3. Newly married men are morons.

4. Cats still hate me. Especially poor little pus-eyed kittens.

5. If you ever see a poor little pus-eyed kitten, just turn and leave.

6. What is funny to a newly married man is often not funny to his newly married wife.

7. Men, learn to say, "Honey, you were right and I was wrong!" Practice it. It won't roll easily off that neophyte tongue at first, but it will come in handy sooner than you think.

8. If you accept money to take a life and dispose of the body, is that a bad thing?

9. If you keep your elbow in, head low, and use a discus spin you can get good distance with a bag of poor little pus-eyed kittens.

10. To this day, my wife fears getting conjunctivitis and finding a house brick and Hessian bag in the trunk of our car.

11. Guys, timing is everything. Never hire out for a hit while you are on your honeymoon.

Life Lesson Number 202

—

"Coming to America"

When you look back on your life, you sometimes wonder what led up to certain major events that changed forever the way that you live. As I sat here today thinking of how we came to be living in America, I started to run down all the obvious reasons that we had given to our families and friends.

Reasons like:

1. We are unable to have children and we won't be able to adopt here in Australia, so we will go to America, adopt a child and live happily ever after. Or

2. I have just finished my bachelor's degree and want to do my master's degree and Dee Ann needs to finish her bachelor's degree, so we will go to America and get educated. Or

3. We have spent the past ten years here, Dee Ann needs to spend some time near her parents, and so we will go to America and be with them for a while.

These were all pretty good reasons for leaving the country of your birth, but none of them were actually true. We didn't "want to leave" Australia, we "had to leave" Australia. Historically this was no different than what happened to my distant relatives. They had been kicked out of some of the best countries in Europe in the early 1800's. We, on the other hand, had to flee.

We had been living in a suburb of Sydney called Marayong. It was a lovely little community of three-bedroom brick houses, filled with single car families, two kids, one dog and cat. Well, that's not absolutely true. We had a three-bedroom brick house, one car, no kids and two dogs. That was what got us into trouble.

My darling wife and I had two dogs that we treated like our children. Nothing could stop us from spoiling them rotten. Honey and Ebony, two beautiful collie dogs, had the best of everything. They were our babies. Life couldn't get any better than this. We had good jobs, a lovely home, two lovely dogs, great neighbors and each other. It was an idyllic situation.

One Saturday morning, my wife let the dogs out the side gate and let them wander as I worked in the front yard trimming edges on the lawn. The dogs were bounding around having a great old time. I smiled as they ran past me trying to get me to play with them. Dee Ann went to the back yard and got a tennis ball for them to chase. She began to throw the ball across the street and down the street. Each time, the dogs would bound off happily to retrieve the bouncing ball and return it to the master to be thrown again.

I finished trimming and started to walk down the driveway to put away my tools. Out of the corner of my eye I saw our neighbor lady from two doors down run out onto the front yard holding her head with both hands and starting to yell. Apparently our dogs had run through her yard and had disturbed her in some way. I heard her yell, "LOOK, IF I WANTED DOGS IN MY YARD I WOULD BUY TWO OF MY OWN!"

Not one who enjoys confrontations such as this, I quietly continued on down the side of the house to put away my tools. It was then that I heard a voice that I did not recognize. It was a rather high-pitched gravelly voice, something like you see those possessed people in the movies using when they want to get attention.

It yelled, "SHUT YOUR FAT FACE!"

When that was said, the neighbor lady yelled back, "WHAT DID YOU JUST SAY!"

I didn't have to wait long for the reply: "YOU HEARD ME, I SAID SHUT YOUR FAT FACE!"

The neighbor lady yelled back, "WELL I NEVER! DID YOU HEAR WHAT SHE SAID TO ME!"

The reply came again, "THAT'S RIGHT, SHUT YOUR FAT FACE!"

After hearing that the neighbor lady apparently gave up and stormed into the house.

I stood quietly in the back yard waiting to see what happened next. I wandered if our neighbor lady really had a fat face and if in fact it needed shutting. Around the corner came my quiet little wife, the woman who had never raised her voice to anyone except her husband. She was red-faced and furious that someone had told her what to do with her dogs.

"Well, that's it," she said, "We have to move!"

And so we did. We sold the house, furniture, and car, packed a few suitcases and moved our bags and both dogs 12,000 miles away from that wicked woman of Marayong.

So what have I learned from this experience?

1.   Small things can have big consequences.

2.   Little packages sometimes pack a big wallop.

3.   Check with your neighbors before you run your animals through their yards.

4.   Love me? Love my dogs.

5.   Exactly how far is far enough away?

6.   You can't write "Dogs Criticized" on the U.S. immigration card asking the reason why you left Australia.

7.   You can criticize me, you can criticize my husband, but if you criticize my dogs, you're done for.

Life Lesson Number 205

—

"Wanna Banana?"

The company that I worked for had for years run a very large mainframe system and had not had much experience with networked PC's. This was about to change. One of the first projects that I worked on in my systems career required us to download large quantities of data from the mainframe to the PC based network each and every night. This data was to be used to generate purchase orders for the inventory that we needed to carry.

Our development team struggled for weeks trying to figure out a fast and reliable method by which we could transfer the large quantities of data required to make our new PC system work. During this period in PC development history there were no direct links available for Mainframes and PC's, so any connectivity had to be achieved through some sort of human interface. Today you can just copy data from one system to the other, but back then it could not be done.

After much research, we found that we could use mainframe backup tape cartridges to dump data from the mainframe. We would then be able to take the mainframe cartridge out of the mainframe tape deck and put it into a special PC based tape deck, which was connected to our network, thus allowing us to load the data to the PC system. All we needed now was to have someone take the tape out of the mainframe tape deck at the right time, put it in the PC tape deck right next to it, and hit a key to load the data to the PC based system. We were off and running. We had a plan, we had a solution, and we were going to be successful.

We required the mainframe support people to load six different tapes each night. If we missed any one of these tapes, our system would not have enough data to create the recommended orders to support the company. Each night's attempt to load the tapes seemed to go wrong. I would get to work in the morning only to find out that tape three had been taken out of the mainframe drive and put on the shelf, or tape five had been misplaced or tape two had been lost. This was no simple task after all. It involved standing in one place, taking out a tape, moving it eighteen inches to the left, placing it in another tape drive, and hitting the enter key. Rocket science, no, but a complex task that appeared to be incapable of being done correctly!

We tried meeting with the staff and talking about the process. We trained. We wrote memos. We made phone calls. Nothing seemed to work. Finally, out of a sense of desperation I did what any frustrated manager would do. I wrote out a purchase order for a spider monkey and a box of bananas.

In the justification section, I noted that this was the only solution that I could see working.

- The tape comes out.
- The spider monkey removes the tape.
- The spider monkey moves the tape and places it in the other tape drive.
- The spider monkey hits the enter key.
- The spider monkey gets a banana.
- I get to sleep in.

I forwarded the purchase order to my boss. To this day I don't know what he did with that purchase order, but for a period of ninety-nine days the humans loaded those tapes correctly and our system was up and running. It was a new record for us.

I guess they ran out of bananas on day one hundred!

So what have I learned from this experience?

1. The simpler the task, the more difficult the concept appears to be.

2. You can always rely on a spider monkey to get the job done.

3. No one wants to be shown up by a spider monkey.

4. Sometimes the not-so-subtle hints work the best.

5. Wait a minute. If the monkey can handle the PC tapes, then the monkey can handle the mainframe tapes! I could be replaced?

6. Repetition does not make you learn unless you really want to learn.

7. It would never have really worked because the spider monkeys would have felt lonely when they didn't get to take a twenty minute smoke break every hour.

Life Lesson Number 207

—

"Wasp Wrong with You?"

We had not been in our new house in Florence for very long when I had my first run-in with American wasps. A large colony had formed a paper nest out under the eve over the garage door and they were proving to be quite annoying. These were rather large wasps with nasty looking stingers that dwarfed any wasp that I could remember seeing in Australia.

Being in a new home and new job with a newborn baby, Tabitha, we were running low on disposable income. When my wife suggested that I get rid of the wasps, I had to come up with a cheap and effective way of disposing of them at no cost. Looking back on my life, I remembered seeing my Dad do something to get rid of a wasp nest at my auntie's house. He had taken a large roll of newspaper, lit it, and held it while it burned up under the nest, thus killing the wasps as they flew out. It was quite effective and so I would try the same thing above my garage.

Having found an old newspaper, I took a few sheets and fashioned an Olympic-like torch that was tightly wound at one end and loose at the other. I took some matches and went out to the garage to take care of the little nasties that were above the door. My wife, bless her heart, must have known what was going to happen, because she stood smiling at the garage door to watch "the show" as she would later call it.

Standing on the ground under the wasp nest, I lit the top of the torch and held it up under the nest smiling at my ingenuity and thrifty solution. It took all of about three seconds for me to figure out that I was in trouble. I noticed that my flaming solution was blackening the vinyl siding (that's right, auntie's house had been solid wood), so I pulled the flame back from the nest. What happened next was like a Japanese Val dive-bomber scene straight out of Tora, Tora, Tora. The wasps in the nest were mildly annoyed at the rise in temperature and decided to seek its source. Having moved the flame back what proved to be a safe distance for the wasps, I gave them a direct route to my head.

Being caught off guard and seeing live wasps coming at my face, I started to swat at the wasps with both my free hand and the flaming roll of paper. Flaming embers started going everywhere, causing me to flash back to certain childhood scenes where I remember having carried a torch similar to the one in my hand now. The swatting and whacking was accompanied by frenzied body spasms as I began to dodge and weave away from the frenzied wasp attack. I had two choices. I could run up the street, but that would look silly, wouldn't it, or I could run into the open garage and shut the garage door to protect myself. I chose the latter.

Having slammed down the garage door I noticed that things were not getting better. I had in fact shut all the following wasps in the garage with me. I now had to run around the car, and swat and dodge all at the same time. In all the running, swatting, whacking and dodging I noticed that my wife was still standing at the door laughing at me. I made for the door, which she quickly opened, and slid through to safety.

She just looked at me, shook her head and said, "What were you thinking?" What could I say to that? I had to agree: "What was I thinking?"

So what have I learned from this experience?

1. Vinyl siding melts when you hold an open flame to it.

2. Wood siding has a higher flame point than vinyl siding.

3. Any normal person would learn from early life experiences not to make flaming paper torches.

4. You can't swat flying wasps with a flaming newspaper.

5. In a wasp attack, given the choice of going for cover in a confined space or running up the street, always run up the street. You can always keep running.

6. The cost of wasp spray is always less than siding repair and medical bills.

Life Lesson Number 210

—

"Let there be Light!"

When you have worked with a bunch of guys for several years and you're all good at your jobs, you start to get a little bored with the everyday humdrum of office life. When this happened to our little group of friends, we started to rely heavily on practical jokes to break the office monotony. One of our running jokes started innocently enough one day over lunch. Somehow the topic of blind people had come up at the lunch table and we marveled at all that they could do nowadays. We had several visually impaired people at work and they were effective associates fulfilling a need for the company.

One of our lunch members did ask an interesting question though: "When blind people go to the toilet, how do they know when to stop wiping?" Now don't get all bent out of shape over this question, because it's a really good question. How do they know? Of course, we spent the rest of the lunch hour trying to figure out how they would know, but none of us could come up with a definitive answer. The question mesmerized our bored minds. We never considered asking any of the blind people at work.

After getting back to the office and starting our afternoon work, I needed to go to the bathroom for some post-lunch relief. As I started for the bathrooms, I noticed that Don, my boss and one of our lunch group, had headed into the toilets ahead of me. I stopped and thought for a moment. Perhaps there is a solution to our lunchtime question. I waited what I thought was an appropriate amount of time, cracked open the bathroom door, noticed that Don's feet were the only feet in the stalls and said, "Don?" "Yes," came the reply that confirmed that I had the right victim. "How does a blind person know when to stop wiping?" I said. "I don't know," said Don. With that I turned off the light, dropping the bathroom into total blackness (it had no windows), and shutting the door I said, "Let me know what you find out!" As the door closed to shouts of "You Mongrel!" I walked off laughing.

Little did I know it, but that one action started a chain of events that would forever change our bathroom habits. As word of my experiment flew amongst our friends, it became the standard joke for each and every one of us to try to catch another member of our group in the bathroom and switch off the lights. If you have ever spent considerable amounts of time sitting in a darkened bathroom, legs numb, feet unresponsive, waiting for someone else to come in and turn the lights on, you would know what I am talking about. The darkness struck terror into our poor little minds.

Things got so bad that a few of us attached small penlight flashlights to our key rings to ensure we had enough light to finish up any paperwork that needed doing. Others of the group set out to try and throw us off their trail by going to bathrooms on different floors. This didn't work because we had set up a network of phone contacts that would call and tell us that Louie was in the second floor bathroom in the three-story building or that Don was up on the third floor for a little piece and quiet. It was all to no avail. We always found them. The hunt was part of the fun. No one could potty in peace.

Things started to fall apart when I made a fatal identification mistake. Walking into the bathroom on the second floor of the three-story building I noticed what appeared to be Don's shoes under the stalls. I had him. Don had sneaked up here for a little peace and quiet. I slapped the lights off and started to walk out. The voice that came from the stall was not Don's; in fact it was the CEO of the company protesting the insult to his dignity. I tried to hurry down the hallway to make my escape but heard the door fling open to the men's bathroom. (The CEO had obviously quickly found an answer to our question) I had only one option: I quickly turned, headed directly for the CEO as if I was on my way to the bathroom, said hello and went into the men's room. It was a brave and effective move. I had covered my tracks.

As the CEO stormed off he was muttering to himself about the idiots who would do such a thing. Within a few days of this incident, almost all the bathrooms had their light switches replaced with motion sensors. Our reign of terror was over. There would always be light.

So what have I learned from this experience?

1. We don't give blind people enough credit for what they have to put up with.

2. Bored adults are just as bad as bored five-year-olds.

3. There is always a scientific test for a reasonable question.

4. People will go to amazing lengths to find a safe and secure bathroom. Some would even drive home.

5. CEO's don't have a sense of humor.

6. I didn't learn from past experiences that shoes do not a person make.

7. We never did learn the answer to our question.

8. At least I didn't kick in the door and sing happy birthday to the guy.

Life Lesson Number 212

—

"The Paperless Office"

I had one particular boss who occasionally gave us some trouble at the office. He wasn't really vindictive; he just didn't think through the consequences of his actions and this caused us to have to scramble on many occasions to fulfill any promises that he might have made to get a deal done.

After he made one particular promise to a client of a service that we didn't really provide, we decided that he needed a little lesson. His office was rather large and had its own small private bathroom. While he was out at a lunch meeting, we sneaked into his office bathroom and removed every, and I mean every, piece of paper from that bathroom. We took the toilet tissue, facial tissues, hand towels, everything. All that was left was one piece of toilet paper attached to an empty roll. We also emptied the garbage can, lest he find any scrap of paper there.

To ensure that our plan worked correctly, we also removed all loose papers from his desk lest he sneak out and put some desk memo to an unintended use. The trap was set. All we needed was the victim to return and take his post-lunch break in the reading room. We could see him now, begging for us to bring him some toilet paper, while we were rolling in laughter at his predicament. We could keep him captive for hours.

When he returned after lunch, he walked through the office jovially greeting the staff and making small talk. As he made his way towards his office, the heads kept popping up over the tops of the cubicles as the staff "prairie dogged" to see what was going to happen. Our anticipation grew as he disappeared into the reading room and shut the door, and so we waited.

After about thirty-five minutes, we realized that he was in trouble. Oh yes, he wasn't going to admit it, but he was definitely in trouble. We needed to up the ante a little, so we rang his office phone and told the secretary not to pick up. The phone rang, and rang, and rang. No boss, no noise, no fuss, no rush to get the phone. We started to get a little worried.

After about forty minutes, we heard the toilet flush, so we all broke for cover. Not a word was spoken as we waited for some comment on his part at the horrible joke that we had played on him. Nothing was ever said, although the secretary did get an email request to have the cleaners restock the tissue in the bathroom. As best we could tell, our boss was lucky enough to have had some small denomination dollar bills in his wallet after lunch. That is the only thing that could have saved him from a fate worse than the embarrassment we had planned for him.

So what have I learned from this experience?

1.   Sometimes people don't even know when a joke has been played on them.

2.   Be kind to your employees and they will be kind to you.

3.   You should always try to carry a good 2-shilling handkerchief.

4.   You should always keep some small denomination notes in your wallet. You might need them for more than tipping.

5.   Bosses can start new office fashion trends. The sockless loafer look might just catch on.

Life Lesson Number 213

—

"Are you paying attention?"

Busy bosses are notorious for asking people to do their work for them. Such was the case with my new boss. He was being torn in many different directions, had not had time to figure out the intricate details of our business, and so relied heavily on me to create the next year's budget.

Never the one to miss an opportunity for a bit of fun, I set to creating a very special budget that would give the new boss a sense of my "rapier-like wit." I had figured out that a lot of my work was just being passed directly on without much review, so I set up a test. In this budget I would create a new title for myself, expand my responsibilities and dramatically increase my salary to a level commensurate with my responsibilities. In the salary budget I changed my position title to Vice President and General Manager, gave myself a twenty five percent pay rise and scheduled the promotion and benefits to begin two months hence.

I was not surprised when the budget came back through approved with all the relevant signatures on it, including the signature of my new boss. I did not say a word. I filed it away, hopped into my Outlook Calendar and entered a reminder in sixty days to process my own promotion.

When the reminder popped up on my calendar, I spent a few minutes putting together a lovely memo to my boss informing him that since "we" had budgeted for my promotion for this month that we should probably begin the paperwork immediately so as to not miss the payroll change cutoffs.

Well, I never thought that I would see someone react so quickly to what was essentially a major oversight on his part. There were probably tread burns on the carpet between his office and mine. During our meeting together to discuss my non-promotion he pointed out that you really shouldn't do things like that in a budget. I almost said, "You really should check things like that in YOUR budget!", but I didn't. I had had enough fun for one day. It was time to move on.

So what have I learned from this experience?

1. If you suspect that people are taking you for granted, test it out.

2. It never hurts to plant a seed of doubt about what might be in the projects you're covering for other people. They tend to read things more closely after an incident like this.

3. If a twenty-five percent pay increase didn't stand out in the budget review, I was definitely not being paid enough.

4. Presidents don't have much of a sense of humor.

5. Take the time to check what other people do for you and thank them for their effort.

Life Lesson Number 215

—

"White men can jump!"

It was a Sunday afternoon in the dead of summer. Dee Ann, Tabitha and Ethan were on their way back from visiting relatives in Texas and I had not picked up the mail from either of Friday or Saturday's deliveries. I had rushed home from church and changed into a T-shirt and shorts to relax for the afternoon prior to the wife and kids getting home. Realizing that I needed to get the mail, I set off down the gravel driveway to the mailbox at the street.

Our house in Florence was on a one-acre lot with a gravel driveway that had a metal culvert at the street to allow water to flow through. This metal culvert had large stones piled on either side of it to stop erosion. It was not pretty, but it was functional. The kids liked to play with the stones to build things and they generally enjoyed using the grassed ditch area as a playground. The mailbox was right next to this stone area.

I made my way gingerly down the gravel driveway to the mailbox in my bare feet. Being the good Aussie that I am, I only wore shoes when I had to, and this was not an occasion when I had to. Having made it to the mailbox, I stood there, opened the box and retrieved about fifty pieces of junk mail and letters that had accumulated over the past several days. As I stood there thoughtlessly categorizing the mail, "Junk, bill, junk, letter, bill," I felt something move over my bare feet.

Looking down I saw a most horrific sight. A three-foot long snake with lots of brown and gold rings was crawling over my feet towards the rock pile of the culvert. Now, I don't know if you know this, but in Australia, if it's a snake, it can kill you. So from years of experience in the land down under, I did what any red-blooded male would do. I screamed like a girl, threw all the mail up into the air, scattering it across the street and into our yard, and jumped straight up in the air to get away from the snake. Why straight up, you might ask? It was as good as any other direction and the one I happened to choose at this critical juncture in time. The jumping and the screaming were apparently accompanied by frenzied arm shaking and flapping.

My neighbor, Roy, saw the whole thing from his front porch rocker. He later told me that he just thought, "Crazy Australian, what is he up to now?" He was impressed by the three-foot vertical leap, but was even more impressed by my "hang time" which apparently was increased by the wild flapping of my arms. In any case, I hung there in space long enough for the snake to make it to the rocks. I, on the other hand, did not hang around when I finally did hit the road again. I bolted up the street fifteen to twenty yards leaving the mail and snake mess behind me. Roy just sat and laughed.

Ok, so I am not the bravest person in the world when it comes to snakes. I did slowly make my way back to the driveway culvert and try to see if I could see the snake. This was not good. The kids would be home in a couple of hours and this was the one place that they liked to play. I had to catch the beast and either remove or kill it prior to their coming home. So off to the shed I went for some tools.

When you hunt snakes you need tools. Preferably long handled tools and the longer the handle, the better the tool. After rummaging around in the shed for a few minutes I found a long handled hoe that gave me a good five feet clearance from the deadly beast. So I set off like a soldier going off to war back to the culvert, hoe over my shoulder.

I stood and stared for a moment to see if I could discern which rock the snake might be under. I couldn't tell if any one stone was better than the other, so I just started to flip the stones back and onto the grass away from the culvert. I flipped the first stone—nothing. I flipped the second stone, threw the hoe across the street, flailed wildly at my face with my hands and ran screaming in circles up the street. I looked like a possessed person beating himself while running uncontrollably in random directions. Roy just sat there and laughed harder.

Our area of Tennessee was prone to have infestations of wasps called yellow jackets. These wasps are unlike any other wasp that I have known because they are small like a bee but extremely fast and accurate in their stings. When I flipped over their rock-hiding place, they became very unhappy with me. Before I could even react, they had shot out of their nest, flown directly for my face, and proceeded to sting me mercilessly—thus the wild arm flailing, random running, and general appearance of possession.

I was humiliated. I looked back down the street. Roy was laughing at me. My mail was spread everywhere. My hoe was flung into the middle of the road and now I could not feel my face. It was as if I had been to the dentist and had several numbing shots. At least the stinging had stopped. Drool ran down my mouth.

I now had two terrible situations to deal with. I had a snake and a yellow jacket nest in the area where my kids played. I had to up the anti, go for the big guns as it were, and get this situation taken care of. I set off back inside to the house, across the yard so as to avoid the new terror, to retrieve the wasp spray from under the sink.

Having made my way back out the front, I realized that I now had more than one person in my audience. Roy now had his wife out the front with him to see what would happen next. Undeterred by their amusement at my situation, I made my way back to the snake/wasp site and prepared to take some critter life. Standing back what I thought was a safe distance I took aim and watched as the initial flow of wasp spray wafted over the nest. This had the effect of annoying the wasps, causing them to, yes you guessed it, buzz out of their hole and chase me up the street one more time. Well, at least I didn't yell this time. My face was too numb. I don't even want to tell you what Roy was doing, but it did involve wiping tears from his eyes.

I realized then what my problem was; just "misting" the wasps did not kill them. They needed a full stream of killer to knock them down. When I finally got the courage up to go back, I emptied the whole can not only on the wasp nest but also all over the rocks on both ends of the culvert. If this stuff was good enough for wasps it might even work on snakes.

Being the good father that I am, I quickly picked up our mail from all over the street, retrieved the hoe, and set off inside to mope and get over my embarrassment. As far as the snake was concerned, if my kids wanted that snake dead, they could do it themselves.

So what have I learned from this experience?

1. White men can jump.

2. NBA Scouts are never around when you need them.

3. Gravity can be defied when jumps are assisted by frantic arm waving movements.

4. Wafted wasp killer just annoys wasps.

5. I scream like a girl.

6. I hate yellow jackets.

7. I hate snakes.

8. Neighbors are often no help at all.

9. There is a direct relationship between the level of embarrassment of a situation and the number of people watching.

10. You can't explain to a laughing neighbor what happened when you have drool running from your mouth, you can't feel you face, and you can't "pronounth yo wodths."

Life Lesson Number 230

—

"Ride Em. Cowboy!"

I lay there flat on my back, gasping for a breath that seemed as if it would never come. The bright lights swirled around me like some ethereal light show beckoning me to the next world. Suddenly, a small blonde female head appeared in the middle of this dream. As she leaned down, the light shone through her golden hair and framed her little face like a little cherubim from heaven. Her lips were moving but I could not hear what she was saying. I was too caught up in the act of trying to breathe. Was she giving me a message from heaven? After a few attempts at getting air into my lungs, I finally succeeded. With that breath, sound resumed in my life.

"Daddy, can I call 911! Please let me call 911," said Tabitha as she leaned over my prostrate form in the middle of our back yard. "Win, wind, winde…Winded!" I tried to say to her as I sucked more air into my expanding lungs. Finally I could get it out, "No, Daddy is just winded and can't breathe properly," I said. "Oh, okay," came the response "that was really cool, what you did then. Can you do it again?" "No honey I don't think I ever want to do that again," I said as I sat up and looked at the mechanical disaster before me.

As I sat there and evaluated myself for injuries, my wife arrived in a state of panic. One of the other kids that were playing in our yard had told her that Mr. Ian was hurt. She knelt down rubbed my back and asked if I were hurt. "No," I said, "Just my pride." When she asked what happened I just responded that this was one of those "Hey Ya'll Watch This" moments in a man's life. You know, one of those moments that any normal person would have seen coming but you barreled into at full steam without even thinking.

Our home in the community of Florence was on a one-acre lot. If you have ever had to push mower an acre of land you would realize that it is quite a task. Being the "boy" that I, am I realized that I needed the "toy" to do the job right. I needed a twelve horsepower, five speed, forty-two inch base, two blade cutting machine that could do this job in forty minutes rather than four hours. So it was that I found myself the proud owner of my first riding lawn mower.

As any red-blooded man will do when given the chance to mix heavy equipment with testosterone, I found myself starting to push the limits. Sure, the user manual tells me that I should mow the lawn in third gear, be careful to apply the brakes during turns, never drive under overhead objects, and never, I repeat, never ever drive that mower on an incline that might tip the mower over. Guys, you know where I'm coming from: when you read instructions like that you want to know why they don't want you to do that. To the testosterone-impaired male mind, the only reason they don't want you to do that is because it is "fun."

So having discarded the safe mowing rules on day one of my purchase, I set out to push the envelope as far as I could. Let me tell you this: I was good. I had that puppy running almost the whole time in fifth gear, blades engaged full speed, throttle wide open, no brake usage at all. I looked like one of those old army jeeps jumping sand hills in "Rat Patrol." Dogs, cats, kids and newspapers lived in fear of getting in my way as I careened around my yard, waving would be victims out of the way, always trying to shave a few more minutes off the cutting time so that I could impress my neighbor friends. I was like the father in the Christmas Story, always wanting to get a tire change time better than five minutes.

After several weeks of getting better times I began to find it harder and harder to shave time off my yard work. As my attempts to reduce the weed eating and cutting time failed, I realized that I could only do one thing to get better. I needed to weed-eat less and mow more. After all you can't weed eat in fifth gear without brakes now, can you? So I had a plan.

I modified my grass cutting angles to allow me to cut around all the trees in the yard on the mower by passing them on only three sides. It was a geometric and mathematical miracle that was only enhanced by the expert driving skills required to make these high speed passes a success. I had one problem though. In the backyard we had a swing set that had three different swings and a slippery slide. This would require some thought.

To the female of the species, the combination of a swing set and mower at high speed would automatically bring visions of death and destruction. To the testosterone-impaired male, it was merely another speed bump on my way to being crowned mowerdom's best and finest.

My plan was to mow the entire back yard, leaving the area around the swing set for the final piece of resistance (as my father used to say). I had made spectacular time on the front and back cuts and was down to a point where I was almost giddy with anticipation at trying out my new "methodology." In my mind the only parts of the swing set that were "fixed in place" were the legs that were driven into the ground. The other dangly bits (swings) moved when you pushed them. Now, anyone should be able to realize that if a person can walk up to a swing and push it out of the way, then a mower could do the same thing.

As I swung into the final straight cut for the yard, I lined up my turn into the swing set. My plan was to drive up to the swing set, apply the brakes to stop just short of the chain link swing, ease forward, push the swing out of the way, then scream off in fifth gear to do it again on the other side. Voila! No weed eating and much improved cutting time!

As I hit the hanging swing, I applied the brake. It was here that adrenalin and testosterone took over and, thinking that the swing had begun to push out of the way, I released the foot brake. As I released the foot brake, the swing caught under the front of the mower. The swing set acted like a fulcrum and as the mower moved forward, the front wheels lifted off the ground by about five inches. Normal sweat turned to cold sweat as I realized that this change in angle was not good.

As the mower raised up at the front, I had to lean forward in the seat to press the brake hard. What followed was a series of futile attempts to balance and stop the process from going bad. I would lean forward, press the brake, causing me to lean backwards, which let off the brake, which moved the mower upward, thus increasing the angle and danger.

When the mower reached a thirty-five-degree angle, I tried a new tactic. The seat in the mower had a kill switch. If you stood up off the seat, the engine would die. While I went through the lean forward, press the brake cycle again, I tried to stand up. Each time I did so, the motor would start to slow down, I would fall back on the seat, and the cycle would start again. Things were getting out of hand.

When the mower reached a fifty-degree angle, I decided that I had two choices. I could ride this puppy all the way or I could hit the silks, bail out, and see how far I could launch this great huge mass of testosterone-impaired manhood from the flailing mower blades. I chose the second option.

With all my might I launched with both legs from the footrests of the mower. As I sailed through the air, I watched as in slow motion the mower (the brake now fully released) continued to spiral up and over. The engine started to die but as the mower tipped over backwards, the seat reengaged the blades. The whop, whop, whopping of the blades continued as the mower crashed back over and tangled in the chains and supports of the swing set.

When I landed on the ground. I landed flat on my back, knocking all the air out of my lungs. I lay there gasping like a beached puffer fish, trying to get air into my lungs so that I would not die. It was then that the little angelic face appeared.

After checking me out to see if I were all right, my wife went back into the house leaving me to survey the accident scene. The mower was wedged upside down and tangled in the play equipment. I hung my head in shame. There could be nothing worse for a red-blooded male than having to admit to himself that he may have done something stupid. I tried to upright the mower. It would not budge. Wait; there is something worse than having to admit to yourself that you have done something stupid! Having to get "other people" to help you fix the stupid thing that you have just done is much worse. I set off to get my neighbor friends.

It took three of us a good thirty minutes to free the mower and get it upright. During that time the guys were pretty good about the whole thing. They did not rib me or give me a hard time at all. They just smiled a lot at each other and went on their way.

After dinner that night I went into the back yard and my neighbors showed up at the side fence to see how I was going. One carried a motorcycle helmet and the other a car safety belt. They didn't have to say a word. Their gifts said it all.

So what have I learned from this experience?

1.   No matter how old they are, boys and their toys will always get into trouble.

2.   I now know how a fish feels when it is out of water.

3.   Testosterone will overcome rational thinking every time.

4.   Gravity bites.

5.   Kids like to dial 911. In some homes they get a lot of practice.

6.   Mowing the yard is a task, not a quest.

7.   You have gone too far if you wear sunglasses, camouflage gear, attach loud speakers to the mower and play Sousa music to get the kids to run from you as you cut.

8.   "Winning" may not be everything, but it's better than "embarrassing."

9. After this, every time I mowed the lawn my neighbors would yell, "Buckle up Bozo!" as they drove past.

10. The "Hey Y'all Watch This!" Hall of Fame has a place reserved just for me.

Life Lesson Number 240

—

"The Tea Party"

One of the benefits of having two children close together is that the older child usually helps make the potty training of the second child easier. Such was the case in our house. I came home one day to find my wife sitting on the bed in our bedroom smiling at our two little naked cherubs in our bathroom.

Rounding the corner to see what she was smiling at, I saw four-year-old Tabitha sitting on the big potty reading her storybook and two-year-old Ethan sitting directly across from her holding a newspaper up pretending to read. This was great; what could go wrong here? We had struggled to train the pupil and now the pupil had become the master; she was training her brother. Life could not get any better than this.

As Tabitha took over the duties of "Master" trainer, we began to relax our hold over "Grasshopper's" training. When Ethan wanted to go to the potty, we would let Tabitha take him. We looked forward to getting him out of those diapers and into "Big Boy's" underwear. The last vestiges of childhood were almost behind him.

When Ethan needed to go, Tabitha would sit on her potty and pretend to read from her book to him. They would giggle and laugh at the stories that Tabitha would make up. All generally had a good time. That is, until the day that the laughter got out of control.

Once again, I found myself in the easy chair watching television. I was quite relaxed and enjoying the moment. In the background I could hear the kids laughing in the bathroom. "No problem!" I said to myself. Tabitha is reading to Ethan and they are having a good time. The laughter and frivolity began to increase in pitch and was now being accompanied by uncontrollable screams of laughter. "What could be wrong?" I thought to myself. Perhaps I should check. As any good father would, I dragged myself from the easy chair and ambled good naturedly up the hallway, smiling to myself at whatever the little cherubs were up to that would cause them such delight.

As I turned the corner into the bathroom, the sight that greeted me caused me to freeze in my steps. The two children were not sitting on their potties. They were both standing, buck naked, in the middle of the two potties, giggling and drinking from small pink teacups. Yes, my friends, it is true. They were drinking from teacups that Tabitha was dutifully filling from the toilet bowl before her. With each dip Ethan and Tabitha wailed with laughter at what they were up to. They had apparently stumbled on the fountain of youth and their parents didn't know about it.

Fortunately they had not seen me, because at this vision of innocent childhood fun I had to clamp a hand over my mouth to stop a gag reflex. I stood there in horror. There could be nothing worse than catching your children drinking out of a toilet.

I was wrong.

Taking one step closer, I noticed that the toilet bowl had not been flushed.

It's at moments like this that you begin to ask yourself, "Ok, where did I go wrong?" Was this happening to me because of the chocolate coconut balls incident early in my life? That's what it was: I deserved this. Turnaround was fair play. Perhaps we were a little lax with the "Master" and "Grasshopper" thing? I struggled with what to do. Dogs drink from the toilet, don't they? We don't spank the dogs for doing that. No, this was different. I knew one thing; these two little imps needed a "handle on the moment." Something that would offset the obvious pleasure they took from drinking out of the toilet. I did what any gagging, retching father would do. I spanked their little pink bottoms. The party was over.

Through their tears, they both looked up at me with tear-reddened eyes and said, "But Daddy, we were just having a tea party!"

"It's not the tea party part that bothers me, Tabitha," I said, "It's what was in the punch bowl!"

So what have I learned from this experience?

1. Sometimes you just need to spank a child as a reference point for change.

2. It's hard to gag and spank at the same time.

3. No matter how many times you flush, plastic tea cups just won't go down.

4. Just when you think things couldn't get any worse, they will.

5. It's hard to replace pink teacups so they match the rest of the set.

6. You get back what you gave early in life.

7. Does this mean my kids will always suffer from "potty mouth?"

8. Supervise, supervise, supervise. That's all I am going to say.

9. Apparently, it's not a real party until someone drinks from the toilet.

Life Lesson Number 241

—

"How big is big?"

Have you ever gone back to the old home place and picked something up that you had as a child and said to yourself, "You know, I remember it being bigger than that?" People ask that question because size can be quite confusing; after all, size is relative. You know how I know that size is relative? I know because my tiny four-year-old daughter taught me that lesson.

It was a lovely Saturday afternoon in the summer and Tabitha, my golden-haired daughter, had accompanied me to the "Quick Lube" store to get our car an oil change. This was a special Daddy/daughter trip. Tabitha loved to tag along and see what the world was all about. She would see things, wonder what they were all about and ask lots of questions that would just make your heart swell with pride at how inquisitive she was.

As is the case in most oil change stores, we left the car to the care of the expert lube men and went into the waiting room to sit down. There is not much to do in a waiting room except sit and read and of course "wait." To an active four-year-old this boring place was just a challenge. To start with, Tabitha smeared her face up against the glass door and watched the men work on the car. She asked some wonderful questions which had the other waiting patrons smiling to themselves and nodding at how cute she was.

Questions like:

"Does that man live down there under the ground?" and
"Why is that man shooting things [pneumatic oil pump] at the car?" and
"Will their Mummies be angry at them for getting dirty at work?"

She was a little joy to behold! She made me so proud.

When Tabitha tired of asking questions, she made her way back and sat down beside me as I read my car magazine. She sat there on the chair beside me, little legs swinging back and forth quietly singing some little song. She was so cute that I could have just hugged her to death.

I read on and smiled as Tabitha continued her singing and leg swinging. It was then that I noticed out of the corner of my eye a lady come in through the door. Now this was no ordinary lady. If you remember from some of our other stories, "I am a big man," so when I tell you that this was a "large lady," I mean "large." I am pretty good at guessing weight and I would have to put her in the 500 to 550 pound range. Strangely enough, all this weight was disproportionately placed in the lower part of her body. Her top half was normal looking, but the rear end was, well, rather large. This largeness was accentuated by the fact that this lady had on stretch pants and a tight T-shirt.

Even as an adult who is trained not to react to these situations I found myself marveling at the breaking strain and engineering feats involved in keeping that much rear end under some sort of clothing control. I berated myself for even thinking that thought and then continued to read my magazine.

It was then that I noticed something. Tabitha's little feet had stopped swinging and the song that she was singing was now silent. Without dropping my magazine, I slyly looked out of the side of my eye and noticed that the sight that was before her had mesmerized Tabitha. The lady had walked up to the counter and then leaned over it to talk to the person behind the counter. This was not a good move. As she leaned over the counter she pushed out her rear end, causing Tabitha to physically pull back in her chair as it loomed ever larger before her. There was still silence from the mesmerized child beside me.

In my mind I started praying the "Daddy's Prayer." You know the one that starts, "Oh Lord, please don't let her say anything that might embarrass me." But it was too late. In slow motion her little right hand started to swing up with a pointing finger. I thought for a brief moment that perhaps with any luck it would continue up to her head and that she might scratch some itch. But it would not be so. It stopped, pointed directly at the woman's large rear end. I shrunk in my chair waiting for the inevitable.

Her little left elbow dug me in my right side. "Daddy?" she said. I ignored her and prayed the Daddy's prayer again. (Except this time I clenched my eyes shut and wrinkled my nose behind the magazine for added effect.) "Daddy?" she said a little more insistently. I ignored her again. The lady at the counter continued to lean and talk. Sweat started to roll down my forehead. I looked across the top of the magazine at the man opposite us and saw in his eyes the same horror that I was experiencing. He, too, knew what was coming. "DADDY!" she finally yelled at me. I could ignore her no longer.

"Yes, Tabby?" I hesitantly asked in a hushed voice. With the little hand still pointing at the largest rear end I have ever seen, she said, "Daddy, that lady has a big bottom!" Well, there it was. Out in the open. No hiding it now. With that statement the large lady at the counter stood bolt upright and froze in place. The clerk behind the counter hurried to busy herself with papers under the desk and the gentleman in the chair across from me hid behind a newspaper that he had grabbed and was apparently reading upside down.

I tried the old "Shhhhh, Tabby, Shhhhhhh," holding a finger to my lips. "Daddy, that lady has a big bottom!" she said again for all to hear. I now had no choice other than to break cover from behind the magazine and address the situation. I tried the indirect route: "Not now, Tabitha!" I whispered forcefully at her. She just looked back at me, started nodding her head knowingly, and said for all to hear, "But Daddy, She has a VERY BIG BOTTOM!" With this final statement, the large lady turned, her eyes burning two laser holes in my forehead, walked across the room, and, turning sideways, she stepped through the door.

Tabitha looked up at me and smiled knowingly as she nodded her little head. You know, she was right.

So what have I learned from this experience?

1.　Kids can go from adorably cute to precociously embarrassing in 6.2 seconds.

2.　People can apparently read upside down when in embarrassing situations.

3.　Desk clerks will always fall back on the old "Oh, I have to get under my desk now to find something" routine, leaving everyone else to suffer.

4.　Sometimes the truth hurts. I have two laser burns to prove it.

5.　If you weigh more than one hundred pounds, just say NO to Spandex.

6.　I now know what Dad meant when he said someone was "two axe handles across the rear end!"

7.　I can never look at saddlebags without thinking of that special day.

8.　I can take solace in the fact that one day it will be MY turn to embarrass my daughter.

9. The Daddy's prayer doesn't work, but I still thank God every day for my daughter.

Life Lesson Number 243

—

"Kitty Litter"

In the future when veterinarian scientists have finally decoded the cat genome, they will make an interesting discovery. In that sector of the cat genome that holds innate species knowledge they will identify a certain gene that will be identified with "species fear." Within that gene there will be specific DNA strands that, when magnified, will show a picture of me. Yes, that's right. Do you know what they will call this gene? They will call it, "The Shepherd Factor!"

Look, it's not that I am unlucky with cats; it's just that cats are unlucky around me. How was I to know that this one lovely summer day in our family history would turn into a catastrophe for us all?

Each summer as my children were growing up we would make the pilgrimage to the great grandparents' farm in Pernell, Oklahoma. It was a lovely farm of about 200 acres, with ponds, cows, ducks, deer, blue herons, turtles, tall grass, barns, tractors, and of course cats. It was a splendid place for a reunion each summer as there were plenty of bedrooms and lots of "farmy things" to do (like shoot guns, step in cow manure, and spit on the ground). From a city boys' perspective, this was a way to get back to my own family roots of farming. It was Greenacres all over again.

This particular summer we met at the farm while my parents-in-law and sister-in-law's family were there. Dan, my brother-in-law, and I had a great time doing all the farmy things that Grandpa would save for us when he knew we were coming in the summer. This particular summer he wanted a small grove of trees chopped down, and as a special treat he had kept the brush hogging (mowing) for us to do. He wanted the farm cleaned up for the winter and we were the muscle to do it.

What more could two burly young men want than to work with chainsaws and heavy equipment? It was a dream-come-true. We would spend the days working through our list of chores, with Grandpa giving directions from the sidelines, and sit around at night talking of our antics from earlier in the day.

Early one morning, Dan set out with the chainsaw and cut down all the small trees that Grandpa had identified as needing to be trimmed. Dan was on a quest to drop them all before I could get out there to help him and take away all the fun. When Dan ran out of the trees that Grandpa had pointed out, he "identified" another small stand not far off from where he was working and so set to leveling them as well.

When Grandpa stepped out on the front porch, he was quite horrified. Dan had cut down his new stand of persimmon trees that were about to bear fruit. I had him now. This was something that I could bring up for years to come at the dinner table as a great comeback like "…yeah, well at least I didn't cut down all of Grandpa's persimmon trees!" I filed this event away in my bag of comebacks for future use.

Later that day Dan and I took turns brush hogging the field out back of the barn. The grass was about 4 feet high and really needed a trim. No matter how hard we tried, we both looked like city slickers sitting on that tractor as it pulled that brush hog. We were in awe of the power with which that 8-foot bed slashed the grass down behind that tractor. The whop, whop, whopping of the brush hog blades sounded just like a helicopter as they devoured the grass before them. We were people of the earth (at least for the weekend).

We had brush hogged the entire field except for one small section near the barn. It was here that a few farm implements had been left: some old tires, a few fence posts, and one of those cow holders that sit in the back of a pickup so that you can transport a single cow to market. It was my turn on the tractor, so I set off on the few last tracks of standing grass. Dan started moving the tires and posts to clear the remaining area to be cut. As I swung by him on the next to last leg of grass, he rolled the metal cow carrier into the already cut area of grass giving me a clear passage to finish the field. Having done this, he stood there leaning on the cow carrier and indicated for me to take one last swing through the tall grass and finish up.

I turned into the last leg and set off on the final run. I felt like the chopper pilot in Apocalypse Now as I bore down on the last section of grass. The only thing missing from the picture was music blaring from speakers hanging out the side of the tractor and the chatter of machine gun fire as I cut a swath of terror through the tall blades of field grass.

I could see Dan smiling out of the corner of my eye. We were about to be done for the day and he was ready to head in to the house. Then, as I passed him,

I heard a scream. Not so much a scream of agony but of terror. It was loud enough for me to hear it over the swooshing of the brush hog blades and the roar of the tractor engine. Looking back (as I had rolled past him), I saw him standing there in horror looking at the ground. Both his hands were raised to the sides of his head and he was holding it as if he needed to stop it from exploding outwards. This concerned me as I thought that perhaps I had hit him with something that had been thrown by the blades.

I quickly stopped the tractor, dismounted, and started to hurry back towards him. He stood there saying, "What are we going to do, what are we going to do?" I thought, "Perhaps a rock has hit him in the head and he is addled." But that was not it. As I drew closer to Dan, I could see a cataclysmic scene that caused me to reel back in horror. Dan was right: what were we to do? He continued to mumble the same thing over and over again in a whispered tone like some mantra recalling the horror from the movie Apocalypse Now.

From a cat's perspective I can probably see why she had picked this lovely place to bring her litter—lots of protection, nice piles of tires, a few fence posts here and there, and, to top it all off, the metal protection of the cow carrier. This was a cat birthing paradise and she planned to use it. Nothing could touch her here. Her litter would be safe and away from those Shepherd children that she so feared. What was it about this family?

Only yesterday she had dragged that one catatonic kitten back from the drinking trough nearly drowned. That little five-year-old Shepherd girl had been baptizing kittens again and had had to pray over the last one since she held it under "a little too long." Thank goodness, her little prayers had worked and the kitten had miraculously revived. They were safe and sound now out of harm's way where nothing could go wrong. That is, they were safe until the large Shepherd took control of the tractor.

As I stood there, I was not so much worried about the catastrophic scene before me, but of how you explain something like this to your wife, children, or anyone else for that matter. I could try something like: "Yes dear, Dan and I had a great day; we cut down some trees, brush hogged the field, moved some farm equipment, mowed eight cats, cleaned the tractor, chopped some wood, and cleaned up around the gate!" Who was I kidding? There is no denying it. She would notice the "eight cat thing" stuck right there in the middle. This unanticipated cat genocide story was going to get out and I would be the "Balkan Monster of Pernell."

Dan and I looked at each other wondering what we should do with the eight dead kittens scattered around us like confetti at a Macy's parade. How could we cover up a mass cat burial site without the family knowing about it? When the next cat count was made, how would we explain the depleted numbers? Just then the decision was made for us.

As we stood there wondering what to do, the mother cat walked up to one of the dead kittens, and as she picked it up she looked at me as if to say, "One day you will pay for this! You are cursed among all catdom!" Turning, she rushed off with the dead kitten to hide it in the pile of fence posts against the shed. She returned and did the same for what remained of each kitten.

As for Dan and me, we both decided that denial and ignorance were the best defense. The mother cat had provided the mass grave. There would be a way out of this. Our position would be "What cats?" or "How many are missing?" or "My goodness, I wonder what happened to them?" So that's how it would be. Deny, deny, and deny for the rest of all time. The worst part of the whole thing was that I could never use the Persimmon tree defense against Dan. He had me, and he knew it.

So what have I learned from this experience?

1. If you are a cat, fear me and fear my children!

2. Cataclysm—a violent event marked by overwhelming upheaval and demolition.

3. Catatonic—a stupor marked by a lack of movement or activity.

4. Catastrophe—a momentous tragic event ranging from extreme misfortune to utter overthrow or ruin.

5. All these words start with "Cat," deal with disaster, and relate to my family. Coincidence? I think not!

6. Five-year-old Shepherd children have a tendency to pay too much attention to cats.

7. Just once in your life you mow eight cats, and people hold that against you for the rest of your life.

8. Hey! At least the litter was baptized!

9. Whenever I hear the word kitty litter, you can guess what flashes before my eyes.

Life Lesson Number 244

—

"Cats and Dogs, living together!"

It was my daughter's eighth birthday and we had just picked up a lovely little white kitten for her. She had always wanted a cat and this would be our first as a family. The cat had two black cookie sized spots on its back, thus the name Oreo (as in cookies) was given to the cute little kitten. How would this lovely, quiet little cat settle in to our hectic household of two adults, two small children and three very large dogs? My wife had a plan.

It is important, she said, to quickly acclimatize the kitten to its surroundings. After a quick tour of the house, the kitten settled down to playing with the kids on the floor. I left the room to take care of something or other and when I returned there is my wife with a wicker open-top picnic basket in her hands. I asked her what she had there.

"I'm taking the kitten out to introduce him to the dogs!" she said. Her plan was to have the kitten in the wicker basket sitting on a lovely white baby pillow while she gently held the package just out of reach of the three collie dogs in our back yard. Never one to want to miss an opportunity for a good giggle, I said, "That sounds like a great idea!", all the while knowing what was going to happen.

We all went out onto the back-porch, children, father, cat and mother. The children and I stayed on the porch so we could see the joy on the kitten's face as he met his new friends. My wife opened the gate, stepped outside and stood ready for the cat to meet the dogs.

The dogs came up to her and seemed excited about what Dee Ann had in the basket. Dee Ann lowered the basket to dog nose height and was about to introduce the cat when things started to get out of hand. Now, my wife did not count on the dogs recognizing the kitten as "A Cat" not "The cat" since this was the first time that they had met.

What ensued was a dance that was a cross between River Dance tap, Olympic high jumping and the Olympic Hammer throw spin, all accompanied by howls and bounding beasts. At the first sniff of the cat, the dogs lunged at the basket. As a reaction to this, my wife held the basket up over her head (with the mistaken thought that if the dogs could not reach the cat, they would go away). She was wrong. The dogs took to standing on their back legs, resting on my wife's shoulders and trying to get at the cat. She held the basket higher until finally it could go no further.

At this point, the dogs did not falter. Realizing they needed extra height, the dogs ran around in a circle, jumped up and pushed off my wife with their front feet and nipped at the bottom of the basket. My wife's composure began to break down at this point. The basket was then used as a weapon to swat at the dogs to keep them away, the kitten in the basket and the introduction apparently forgotten.

The kitten, knowing that its new owners had brought it out here to feed it to these beasts, decided that if it were going to die it would take someone with it. The kitten sank its claws into something to hold on to, and that just happened to be the free hand of my wife as she tried to hold the cat in the flailing basket. My wife began to scream, the cat began to howl and the dogs began to growl. The flailing basket arced through the air with the little kitten in a gravity-defying spin.

It was at this point that a bright yellow substance began to squirt out of the basket. The cat had had enough. It was obviously frightened to death. After much flailing, jumping and whacking, Dee Ann finally made it back up onto the porch with muddy paw prints and cat poop all over her.

"That went well!" I exclaimed.

She said, "You know, I had always heard that you could have the poop scared out of you!" and she broke down laughing.

I started to say "What were you thinking..." but I was cut off by "the don't you dare go there look." So I didn't.

So what have I learned from this experience?

1. Dogs don't know the difference between "A Cat" and "The cat." Cats are just cats.

2. This was my first use of the line "What were you thinking!" It would not be the last use, as history would show.

3. A cat will stay in a basket just like water will stay in a bucket as you spin it around.

4. You <u>can</u> scare the poop out of someone.

5. The speed of the spin is directly proportional to the pitch of a cat's howl.

Life Lesson Number 245

—

"The Cat is a Hat!"

Never one to be discouraged by failure, my wife continued to work at acclimatizing the new kitten to our three very large collie dogs. After several weeks of barking, hissing, clawing and growling, things started to settle down to some semblance of order in our house. Well, I wouldn't exactly use the word "order," but perhaps the phrase "uneasy truce" might be more appropriate. With each introduction, the dogs began to recognize the kitten as "the cat" not "a cat" and thus they began to tolerate each other's presence.

On the rare occasion when the dogs were in the house and the cat was around it was like watching an old western movie. It was one of those scenes where the sheriff and the bad guys eye each other off and move slowly in circles while trying to get the drop on the other party. It was the old "I see you there, so don't make any fast moves or you're done for!" slow dance that often led to a disastrous end. The dogs appeared to be learning the difference between "the cat" and "a cat" and that was all that mattered to us. It was quite a relief.

In the back yard, however, it was a different story. Any cat that wandered in was dutifully chased, treed and abused with much barking, jumping and growling. The dogs would try their best to get to those cats. They would even jump up and off the trunks of the trees trying to get to those annoying beasts.

The cats, of course, knew what was going on and, I believe, knew exactly where on the branch they needed to sit so as to drive the dogs wild and yet be just out of reach. The dogs, frustrated in their attempts to get the cat, would thrash themselves into a foaming frenzy and eventually collapse exhausted in the shade of the tree. In their exhausted pose, the dogs never faced the cat lest the cat sense that it had been victorious over the dogs. Eventually the cat would leave out of boredom, leaving the dogs to sleep.

My son Ethan, who was about four years old at the time, did not like the dogs chasing the neighborhood cats in the back yard. When the melee began, he would run yelling into the house calling for help to stop the frenzied attack. Ethan had a soft spot for animals and wondered why "they all just couldn't get along!"

Being four, skinny, and small was quite daunting to Ethan. The dogs were much larger and rougher than he liked and the cats had claws and teeth. The thought of him trying to stop the fights just terrified him. He had visions of himself being mauled by any such intervention.

Late one Saturday afternoon we discovered what made the difference between "the cat" and "a cat." The dogs and kitten were in the house and they were doing "the slow gunslinger circle" around each other. You could tell that neither species trusted the other and that any unsuspecting move could set off a situation that could quickly get out of control.

I sat in my easy chair and watched the slow dance unfolding before me. Just then, Ethan ran innocently into the room. His entry caught the kitten off guard and caused it to make a near fatal mistake. It broke from its sloth-like walking motion, broke eye contact with the dogs, and darted into the kitchen. There it was: the difference between "the cat" and "a cat" was the speed of the cat.

The three dogs took off like a freight train after the kitten. The growling, barking, hissing and howling were intense. The dogs followed that kitten around the kitchen table at rates of speed approaching a blur.

I was amazed at how much noise three dogs and a kitten could make. Then it struck me, somewhere in all that barking, howling and hissing was a high-pitched small boy scream. It was Ethan. The sight of the doggy freight train barreling down on the kitten caboose was too much for him. He knew that he needed to get out of the way and let the adults take care of this situation, but where to go? "Oh look, a chair!" he thought, "I will be safe up there!" So bounding out of the way of the careening dogs, Ethan jumped onto the kitchen chair and stood there, hands held stiffly by his side screaming for help.

The kitten and dogs were of course oblivious to Ethan's situation. This was about to change though, because two laps around the table later the cat realized, "This ain't working! I need some height to give me the advantage!" The kitten then did what any self-respecting hunted raccoon would do, and went for the high ground. Unfortunately that high ground was my son, standing erect on a kitchen chair, his head now being the highest point in the room.

The kitten circumnavigated Ethan about three times as he clawed his way up the chair and around his body finally settling on the back of his head like a cat skull cap. Having reached what it thought was a place "safe from the dogs," the kitten then dug his claws into the forehead and throat of my son and hung on for dear life. It looked like Ethan had on a Davy Crocket Cat Skin hat except that the hat was still alive.

Needless to say, the human wailing grew louder and was now accompanied by head thrashing as Ethan tried to dislodge the kitten from the top of his head. With each shake, the kitten would just jam its claws deeper into Ethan's skin causing more anguish and thrashing. As Ethan thrashed, the cat hissed and howled. Things were getting interesting.

It was at this point that the dogs, realizing they had treed "a cat," set to jumping up and pushing off the trunk of the tree before them. Unfortunately, that trunk was my son. The dogs would pounce, my son would wince at the thump of their paws and bend at the waist, which lowered the cat towards the dogs, which in turn caused the cat to claw tighter at his head, thus causing him to scream and stand stiffly erect. Someone had to break this cycle of madness and mayhem. I guess it had to be me.

I hurried into the kitchen, grabbed the three dogs' collars and hauled the bounding beasts out through the back door. The noise was terrible. The dogs were barking outside. The cat was howling and attached to my son's head. My son was still screaming for someone to help him. I hurried back inside and standing behind him grabbed the kitten by its stomach and tried to pull it off his head. With each pull the kitten, sure I was going to throw it to the dogs, jammed its claws further into my son's forehead and throat. Each pull was associated with a synchronized howl from both the kitten and child. This was not getting any better. I had replaced the dogs in this frenzied farce.

It finally struck me that I should give up the idea of gently supporting the small kitten by the stomach and just pry its legs loose letting it fall to the ground. This worked. The cat hit the floor and was gone.

Ethan turned around with a bloodied forehead and throat and tear covered face and demanded to know why I hadn't helped him sooner. What could I say? The sight of a small boy with a live Davy Crocket cat skin hat had awestruck me. It was "a pet train wreck" for all-intents and purposes and I just couldn't take my eyes off the scene.

So what have I learned from this experience?

1. Cats are mean and take pleasure in taunting dogs.

2. Dogs can be as dumb as a bag of hammers.

3. The real difference between "A Cat" and "The Cat" is the speed of the cat.

4. A father's reaction time is inversely proportional to the humor found in the situation before him. The funnier it is, the slower you react.

5. The pitch of the synchronized howl is determined by how hard you pull the cat.

6. Never assume that the high ground is the safest place to be.

Life Lesson Number 247

—

"A close shave!"

The fur was flying in the breeze. It was in my mouth, in my eyes, and all over my clothes. Hairballs were going everywhere. If this were a shearing competition, then I was determined to win it. The other three animals that I had just shaved were no match for my innate Aussie shearing skills. I had subdued their pitiful lamb-like efforts to pull free and had shorn them clean for the summer. Why should this little beast be any different?

I don't know what possessed me to do it. Perhaps it was because I was on a roll? Perhaps it was because the beast had been shedding all over the house and its fur was stuck to everything and anything that had static cling? Perhaps it was because I knew the beast would not like it? Vindictive, maybe, but the solution was practical nonetheless. No fur equaled no shedding and no shedding was a good thing. That cat's fur was coming off whether the cat wanted it to or not.

Now when you shear large animals like collie dogs you can hold them like a shearer holds his sheep. You can leg lock them or position them to give you good clear cutting lines. You can't do that with a cat. Cats tend not to stand still while you scrape electrical equipment over their bodies and tear off their fur. Having begun this process with our cat, it occurred to me that cat shearing should be an Olympic event. It would rival the thrills of Greco Roman wrestling but have extra degrees of difficulty brought about by the high voltage electrical equipment involved and the fierce nature of the beast being subdued. In my mind I was blazing new sports horizons.

I had started with the cat's tail. Why the tail you might ask? Well, the tail is the obvious place to start because you can hold on to it (as I learned early in life) and shave it as the frenzied cat tries to run away from you. This is how I handled much of the cat shaving process. I held the tail, pushed the electric clippers towards the cat's head, and as the buzzing beast approached the cat's head, the cat tried to claw itself away from the approaching death machine. I used the cats fear to get the job done. Needless to say, the sound that a cat makes while you hold its tail and shear it is not a pretty one. With each forward stroke of the clippers, the cat would pull away, thus meeting resistance at his tail, which caused the cat to howl its displeasure at the situation.

Things went pretty well until I had shaved two-thirds of the cat. I had gotten up to the back of the neck and down around his two front legs done. He looked like a white lion with a large white mane. The rest of his naked little body reminded me of a Chihuahua. His pencil-like tail whipped around as he tried to free himself from my grasp.

The shearing process broke down when I reached the cat's front shoulders. The cat had obviously had enough and had determined that if he were going to be devoured by the buzzing beast that was removing his fur then, he would take the buzzing beast with him. With each attempt to shave above the cat's shoulders, it would turn around, bite the clippers or electrical cord, and attempt to sever the hand that held them. We had reached a shearing impasse. The cat's nerves were frayed, to say the least, and his tail had been held long enough.

My work here was done. Sure, the cat was only two-thirds shaved, but I felt like a new man. It was one of the most therapeutic things I have ever done. It's not often that you get to get your own back on the cat that sits on your face while you sleep, or sprays in your closet, or vomits on your bed, or rubs his whiskers on your nose while you sleep. As far as I was concerned, turnaround was fair play.

So what have I learned from this experience?

1. You can shave a cat, but it won't like it.

2. Unlike poodles, you can't be stylishly creative when you shave a cat. Patterns are out and a bouffant look is impossible.

3. Cats hold grudges.

4. Cat Shaving as an Olympic event? I vote yes!

5. Someone should start cat shaving therapy sessions for frustrated cat owners.

6. There is only one thing scarier than waking up with a cat's bottom sitting on your face. That's right, waking up with a shaved cat's bottom sitting on your face.

Life Lesson Number 251

—

"Whack a Mouse"

She stood there screaming with her little hands stretched out begging for help. The dead mouse was sitting fair smack in the middle of her golden hair. Her brother had caught sight of what had happened and had high-tailed it inside to get her mother. This was not going as I had planned. I could see in Tabitha's eyes that this was a serious infraction on her personal space and that I would probably be paying for therapy in years to come for this little incident.

It was the summer of 1994 and we had been having the worst dry spell in years. The drought had dragged on for months. The grass was dying. The dogs were hot and bothered and for the first time ever we began to have mouse problems. It was easy to see that the field mice from the farm behind us had found that our dogs were being fed and watered every day with supplies from our shed. Having made this discovery, they decided to set up shop, settle in, and make a little community out of it. The dogs didn't mind, and for the most part I didn't mind until one Friday night.

Tabitha loved to camp out. Well, not really camp out. She had her little Barbie sleeping bag and she liked to use it a lot. So occasionally we would sleep on the den floor. She was not ready to actually "go outside." The den floor was close enough to "camping" for her.

We were both asleep in our sleeping bags on the floor when Tabitha woke and said, "Daddy, the cat is sitting on me and he has something!" I got out of my sleeping bag, put on the light, and, sure enough, there was Oreo the cat sitting on Tabitha's sleeping bag, throwing a dead mouse up in the air. The mouse would land on the bag. The cat would look at you as if to say, "See what I can do?", then pick up the mouse and throw it up in the air again. I must say that I was actually impressed that this psycho cat had actually caught something.

After a few minutes of enjoying the scene, I snatched the mouse by the tail, thus depriving Oreo of the tasty morsel he had caught. I took it to the bathroom and flushed it. With that done, both Tabitha and I settled back in for a good night's rest.

About an hour latter I woke up with the cat sitting squarely on my chest, its face about six inches from mine. The sitting was accompanied by low growls. I asked Tabitha to get up and turn on the light. When she did, we could see that the cat now had a live mouse in its mouth. The mouse's head was poking out and its little nose whiskers were swishing as it frantically tried to extricate itself from the cat's mouth.

"Enough is too much foolishness!" I thought and got up to free the mouse, dispose of it, and get back to sleep as soon as possible. This would not be an easy task. The cat did not want to give up the mouse. He had seen me flush the other tasty morsel and this one was not going to go down the gurgler with the other. After about fifteen minutes of chasing, grabbing, prying and stumbling, the cat released the still live mouse from its deadly jaws.

When the mouse hit the floor, it started to scamper away. The cat took off after it, I took off after the cat, and Tabitha laughed with glee at the chase. The mouse made for a corner of the room and thought that it had made it to safety. As I passed by the couch I picked up one of the kids' large plastic air-filled softball bats and whacked the mouse. It was dead and Tabitha was delighted with the chase and the outcome. The cat, of course, slunk away in shame at having lost another tasty tidbit down the tubes.

So we had a mouse problem. That was obvious. What to do about it was the next question. The next day, Tabitha, Ethan and I went out to the shed to see if the mice were in there. As I opened the door mice scattered everywhere. Tabitha and Ethan were amazed! They had never seen that many mice in all their lives. I said, "We will never catch all these mice with traps" to Tabby and she responded with, "Why do we have to catch them? Let's bop them with the bats!"

I liked this girl; she was thinking like her five-year-old father used to think. I guess the apple doesn't fall far from the tree.

With that decision made, we shut the doors until we could get three big bats. When we came back outside, we threw open the doors again and set to playing "whack a mouse." I was so proud to see both Tabitha and Ethan hammering on the mice. What better way for a family to pull together than this! The first day we killed twelve. At the end of the frenzy I could see the blood lust in their eyes. They wanted more of this. It was real fun. We were three tired gladiators ambling home after the kill.

For the next few weeks we would wait for the weekend and then after dinner on Friday, we would go outside to "Whack the Mice." All was well. The kids' swings were really coming in and the count was: Shepherds—Thirty Five, Mice—Zero.

Having worked our way through the colony in the shed, we were now working on the last vestiges of mouse civilization under the doghouses. I had stepped back from my duties of chief mouse whacker and now I just tilted the doghouses back and watched as my kids pounded the furry little beasts into oblivion.

It was during one of these sessions that it all went wrong. In a horrific accident of timing, my two mouse-whacking kids had somehow gotten out of sync in their swings. The two bats caught and Ethan's upswing threw off Tabitha's downswing. Well, rhythms got all fouled up and one bat smashed down upon another bat already on a mouse.

What happened next, happened in slow motion. As the upswing of the bottom bat began, the double whacked mouse "stuck" to the bat. At least it did until it reached the top of the arc in the swing. At that point, the dead mouse "goo" failed to hold the mouse onto the bat. As it left the bat it could have flown anywhere else in the yard, but it didn't. It went straight up in the air and then landed right in the middle of my daughter's head.

Game over. It was an obvious victory for the mice.

Shepherds—Forty Two, Mice—One—but that's all it took. We never played whack a mouse again.

So what have I learned from this experience?

1. The apple doesn't fall far from the tree.

2. Cats play with their food.

3. You can be really creative with your family activities.

4. It's not how high the score is in the game, it's who scores last that really counts.

5. Timing is everything in "Whack a Mouse."

6. Its all fun and games until the dead mouse lands on your head.

Life Lesson Number 266

—

"Jet Ski Waikiki!"

In 1996 we decided to meet my parents and sister in Hawaii for a week's vacation. It was going to be our first real vacation together as a family when we did not actually go to a family members' house. We were really looking forward to the relaxing time that we would have. Susan, my sister, was engaged to be married and had asked her fiancée Mark to come along as well. So we had four hotel rooms to ourselves and settled in to enjoy our relaxing week.

We spent the first few days seeing the beautiful sights and walking along the beach, as well as visiting the touristy shopping area to buy some goodies to take home with us. It was during one of these walks that my sister saw a sign that said, "Jet Ski Rides—$50 for one hour." What a great deal, she thought. When we got back to the hotel, Susan convinced Mark and me that we had to go on the Jet Ski Ride because it would be a real "adventure."

Based on my previous experiences with "adventure" I should have declined this little trip and stayed in the hotel room, but, no, my mother and wife convinced me that I should go "for the experience." After all, how often do you get to Jet Ski in Hawaii?

So it was that the three of us put on our swimmers and thongs (flip flops) and made our way down to the beach. As we walked up to the Jet Ski Cabana that sat on the beach, I noticed that there were few patrons hanging around. This, however, did not deter me. We joked amongst ourselves, signed the waivers without reading them, paid the $50, and waited for instructions.

I don't know if your family has a measure of concern for certain activities or events, but in our family we have settled on a rather imprecise and scientifically un-measurable scale called the Pucker Factor. This scale has a subjective scale of zero to ten with zero being completely relaxed and ten representing a person's stress and physical reaction at the moment they realize they face a horrible agonizing painful death. It is somewhat akin to the "Hey ya'll watch this!" factor that is used in Southern America by the male of the species as they dare each other on to more dangerous acts.

Pucker Factor=0 (Calm and content—life is good.)

It was at this point that I turned around and looked down the beach. "Sue," I said, "Where are the Jet Skis?" Sue didn't have to answer; the cabana boy behind the counter jumped in and said, "Oh, they're not here. Let me explain the procedures for you to ride them." At the first mention of "procedures" I felt a little uneasy. It is a well known fact that I am deathly afraid of large salt-water beasts that might eat me. I can barely get out any deeper than my waist if there is clear open-ocean between me and the beasts of the deep. As I looked at the open ocean, I decided that "this procedure" sounded like something that might be dangerous.

Pucker Factor=1 (Apprehensive—life is scary.)

The cabana boy stepped out of the cabana and walked us down the beach to the water's edge where there were two double seat surf skis waiting. It was here that he imparted to us the quest that we had set ourselves upon.

"Here's what I want you to do," he said. "Grab yourselves a surf ski and life-jacket and row out to that buoy you see about a mile offshore there. When you get there, tie off to the buoy and wait for the Shark Cat to come pick you up!"

Pucker Factor=2 (Concerned—my life may be in danger.)

The combination of "Surf Ski," "Row," "One Mile," "Buoy," and "Shark Cat" caused me some consternation. It was now that I tried to get some sort of sane answer to the question of what we had just signed up for. I asked, "Where are the jet skis?", thinking that the cabana boy would say "Down the beach," but I was wrong. He then told us that they keep the Jet Skis about five miles out in the open ocean. That's as close as they could bring them to Waikiki beach. My hopes were dashed. I was about to die for sure and it was all my sister's fault for signing me up.

Pucker Factor=3 (Deeply concerned—my life "is" in danger)

As the cabana boy left, I donned my life jacket (which of course did not fit) and looked at Mark and Sue as they dragged their surf ski into the ocean. Fear overcame me as I realized that they were leaving me behind. So I jumped on the surf ski and struck out after them, sure that certain death was just below the surface. After a few strokes and one or two small waves, we started to joke about how bad could this really be? We set off for the real breaker line at the edge of the reef.

I don't know if you have ever ridden a surf ski, but it is a long and low surfboard that is barely hip wide. To balance it requires hip and lower back movements similar to those required for the hula. To say the least, these modes of transportation are quite unstable. Add to this instability the great huge body mass of an out-of-condition office worker trying to dislodge itself over either side and you have a recipe for severe lower back trauma. About one hundred yards offshore my back started to ache like someone was stabbing me with a knife. I pressed on. I started to harbor ill will towards my sister for bringing me here. This was supposed to be fun, not painful.

Pucker Factor=4 (Extreme Worry—what else could go wrong?)

About three hundred yards out from the beach the first white water hit the front of my surf ski and upended me into the water. Susan swears that I popped out of that water and back onto the surf ski like a jack out of its box. All I know is that if the sharks were going to get me they would have to get me off the top of the surf ski. I pressed on through the white water, falling in at least three times. Each time it became more difficult to launch myself vertically out of the water and back onto the surf ski. I was already exhausted and barely could lift my arms to row.

Pucker Factor=5 (Physical Illness—nature's way of telling you you're stupid).

Having finally made it past the breakers, we set out on the three-quarter-mile row out to the buoy where we were supposed to tie up. As the water turned from clear to light blue I started to mention to Susan that perhaps we should turn around, forget the $50, and go back in. She made me press on. Mark was having a good time and he thought that there weren't any sharks around. The mention of sharks makes me physically ill. My mouth dried out, my stomach started to gurgle and my back was about to break in two. My bottom cheeks burned from the exertion of trying clench the surf ski to gain some sort of stability.

Pucker Factor=6 (Resignation—death comes to those who wait)

When we finally made it to the buoy, we tied up and waited and waited and waited. With each passing minute I was absolutely sure that they had forgotten us and that we would be out here at dark just as the feeding frenzy was about to start. After what seemed like forever I could hear the sound of an outboard motor way off in the distance. It was the Shark Cat and they had come to rescue me.

As the Shark Cat pulled alongside the buoy, the crewman asked us to jump into the boat. Now, for any normal sized person, that would not be a problem. For me, it was a task fraught with terror. I had to drag myself off the surf ski and over the side of this large boat without dangling any bait in the water. Not an easy task. My future brother-in-law eventually gave me a bit of a hand over the side of the boat and onto the floor and so we were off to the Jet Ski area.

The big Shark Cat turned and headed off at full throttle directly out to sea. I sat there in the back of the boat looking back at the Waikiki beachfront as it shrunk in size. Buildings that were really big when you looked back from the buoy were now half an inch high. I know how high they were because I sat there measuring them between open fingers, trying to figure how far we would have to swim when attacking great white sharks holed this boat. The ocean changed from light blue to dark blue to black.

Pucker Factor=7 (Sheer Panic—usually accompanied by loss of bowl and bladder control)

As the engines stopped, I could see a line of Jet Skis tied off to another ocean buoy about twenty feet from the Shark Cat. This line of Jet Skis floated off for quite some distance. After a moment of hesitation I asked the large Hawaiian man if they were going to get the Jet Skis for me. He said, "No, you just jump in, swim over, climb up and start the ski yourself."

Pucker Factor=8 (Self Preservation—Primal instinct for survival takes over)

As I looked at the black open ocean, the 20 feet to the nearest Jet Ski and then my sister, all I could hear in my head was the theme from Jaws. Had there not been any witnesses I might have thrust myself upon Susan and strangled her with her bathing suit strap. But that would not work. How could I get back at her? There was obviously only one way. I had to be the first one over the side, make it to the nearest Jet Ski, and thus give her the greatest chance of death by shark munching. This was a workable plan.

I can still see the funny look on Susan's face as I bolted like a rat out of a sewer pipe over the side of the boat. She knew I was horrified of sharks and wondered what I was up to. Self-preservation, that's what I was up to. I made it to that first Jet Ski almost walking on the water. When I got to the Jet Ski I realized that I didn't know how to get on. This would have been an important piece of information to gather before thrusting oneself into the feeding grounds of man's only true predator. Each time I tried to get up on the Jet Ski it would roll over and throw me back into the water.

Pucker Factor=9 (Paralytic Fear takes over, you lose control of outer extremities)

After several minutes of wallowing at the back of the Jet Ski like a giant Orca whale trying to mate with an over-inflated inner tube, I finally broke down and had to ask for help. The Hawaiian man jumped in and held the front steady while I mounted my trusty steed. As I started the motor and began to set off away from the Shark Cat I asked what would happen if I fell off. The man yelled back "You're on your own!" "Well, that's just great isn't it," I thought to myself. I reasoned that if I actually went any faster than idle that I would fall off and surely die a horrid munching death. Worse still, I might even fall off and wallow at the back of the Jet Ski with the Hawaiian guys laughing at me and then have that topped off by being eaten by great whites.

Pucker Factor=10 (Near Death Experience)

For the next hour, I tootled around the course at a snail's pace while my sister and future brother-in-law raced past me making fun of my fear. Even at my slow speed the pounding of the Jet Ski over the large swell caused my rear end much discomfort. My one consolation was that, while racing around, Mark jammed his toe into the jet ski while jumping a wave and Susan was suffering from the worst swimwear wedge ever known to mankind. There was some justice to all this. The blood in the water from Mark's stubbed toe only caused me greater anguish. In my mind I could see those great white beasts homing in down the chum trail of blood only to find me in the water rather than Mark.

As our time on the Jet Skis came to an end I realized that I now had to do the whole process in reverse. I began to think that perhaps there was a chance that I might make it back alive after all. I had made it this far—what else could go wrong?

Pucker Factor=9 (Paralytic Fear takes over, extremities regain some movement)

The greatest difficulty I faced was of course transferring my hugeness from the Jet Ski into the Shark Cat; this was achieved by ramming the side of the boat and jumping off as I passed by the boat at high speed. I did not care what happened to the Jet Ski; it could float free for all I cared. I was safe on board, prostrate on the floor, kissing the bottom of the boat. When we set off for the buoy, I sat up and tried to regain my strength.

Pucker Factor=8 (Self Preservation—Primal instinct for survival takes over, usually accompanied by a lack of concern for inanimate objects)

The transfer from the Shark Cat to the surf ski went more smoothly than I expected, thanks to the helping hands of our Hawaiian boatmen. The process was not unlike those shows where you see the "Save the Whales" guys transferring an Orca whale by canvas sling from the back of a pickup truck into the water. The process I went through was much the same with lots of groaning, lifting and lowering of a large dangerous mass into a fluid environment, the only difference being the Hawaiian guys didn't have T-shirts that said, "Save the Australian."

Pucker Factor=7 (Sheer Panic—definitely accompanied by loss of bowl and bladder control)

After getting back on the surf ski and setting off for the long row back to shore, the trek didn't seem all that bad. I had made it this far and lived—what else could go wrong? While we were out, the swells had picked up a little and the white water over the reef had one more chance at killing me. I bravely made for the breakers, hoping to make it through safely. It would not be so. After falling off four or five times I finally gave in. I floated beside the surf ski like a big piece of chum cast from a fishing trawler, willing the sharks to "Just take me now and put me out of my misery!" I just didn't have the strength to get back on the surf ski.

Pucker Factor=6 (Resignation—death comes to those who float and wait)

As Mark and Susan waited for me, Susan said, "What are you doing?" So I told her that I was waiting to die. She just laughed and told me to stand up and walk the rest of the way in. It was the ocean's one last cruel joke on me. The tide had gone out and my theatrics were for naught.

Pucker Factor=5 (Physical Illness caused by mental stress—natures way of telling you you're stupid).

To this day I have never gotten over the experience I have just described to you. As far as the pucker factor is concerned, I took it all the way from 0 to 10 and almost made it back past 5. I have been stuck at 5 ever since.

So what have I learned from this experience?

1. Always read the fine print.

2. Never trust a cabana boy.

3. For that matter, you should probably never trust your sister.

4. Never ask yourself how bad could this be, because it will always get worse.

5. I now know how frustrated a sperm whale can be.

6. The need for self-preservation will overcome brotherly love any day.

7. I will always be able to recognize an atomic bathing suit wedge from a distance.

8. The pounding of an open ocean Jet Ski ride does cure a bad case of hemorrhoids.

9. When it comes to the pucker factor, you can take it from 0 to 10 but you can never go back to 0.

10. I now know how my bait feels when I fish.

11. No matter how hard and how often you clench your bottom cheeks, they will not keep you on a surf ski.

Life Lesson Number 256

—

"Say it isn't so Mommy!"

Christmas at our house always had that comfortable routine about it. We had our small family rituals that we would observe each year on Christmas Eve. The kids would bathe early, put on their red pajamas and then write letters to Santa Claus telling him how they had behaved each year. We would then gather around the fireplace and I would read "The Night Before Christmas" to them.

In preparation for Santa's arrival Tabitha would prepare milk and cookies on a plate while Ethan gathered a small number of baby carrots for the reindeer to eat. The letters from the children would be carefully placed next to the milk and cookies so that Santa could not possibly miss these important communications regarding behavior throughout the last year. Prior to heading off to bed, Tabitha and Ethan would check that their stockings were hanging over the fireplace and visible from the cookie stash in the kitchen.

Christmas of 1999 would start out no different from the others. As parents, our Christmas preparations were long and hard. By the time we carefully kissed the foreheads of our ten-year-old daughter and eight-year-old son as they snuggled in their warm beds, we were exhausted.

As we had in the past, we would wait until later in the evening for Santa to make his appearance and place the presents lovingly under the beautiful tree. We were ready, but the children were not asleep. Taking this time as a gift in an otherwise busy day, I made my wife a hot cup of cocoa, left her watching TV, and went to take a long hot bath in our Jacuzzi tub.

What a wonderful and memorable evening it had been! Parents long for Christmases such as this. This was one Christmas I would look back on and remember the pure innocence and acceptance of our children as they eagerly anticipated the arrival of old Saint Nick. With the children getting older, there may not be many more Christmas Eve's like this.

At first I thought that the heat of the hot tub and the bubbling water were playing tricks on my ears. I could hear disturbing noises coming from the TV room at the bottom of the stairs. I dismissed them at first as TV noise and wondered why my wife would be watching a show so loudly, and especially one where children appeared to be crying hysterically. Goodness knows that Dee Ann would never want to wake the children, especially on this night of nights. I closed my eyes tighter, sank a little deeper into the bubbling water and wished that Dee Ann would turn the TV down.

Oddly enough, the noise didn't abate. In fact, it appeared to get louder and louder. The ruckus finally reached a point where I decided that I needed to get out of the tub, dress, and let Dee Ann know that she needed to quiet down lest she wake the children. So I dressed and made my way to the TV room.

The scene that met me caused me to freeze in place. On the couch facing the stairs sat Dee Ann crying. On the lower stairs sat Ethan hysterically crying and holding his head in grief. Just above Ethan sat Tabitha, crying just as loudly and obviously quite shaken by the grief being shown in the room.

I struggled at first to take in the enormity of the situation. Just a few minutes ago, we had smiling, rosy-cheeked children chasing sugarplums in their sleepy heads. Now we had three hysterical people moaning and crying as if I had died and left them penniless. After a few moments of trying to gather my thoughts, I looked at my wife and calmly said; "Did I miss something?"

Since we had been married for twenty years, the look I got from my wife was not lost on me. As Dee Ann's eyes burned through me she stated the source of the hysteria. "I just told the children that there is no Santa Claus!"

At this repetition of the revocation of their innocence, both Tabitha and Ethan wailed louder.

In hindsight, perhaps my response was abrupt and probably tempered by the timing of the revelation. It also could have been the short amount of time I had to take in the scene before me. I responded with: "Why on earth would you do that? It's Christmas!"

Raised and outstretched arms accompanied this statement as I reached towards heaven for guidance under such dire circumstances. As smart as my children are, they did not miss the confirmation of their mother's statement in my question to her. The wailing became louder and more pronounced.

Ignoring the children as best I could, I waited for a response. "Because they asked me!" replied Dee Ann.

At this point Ethan began to chime into the discussion with a few zingers like: "I can't believe that the whole Christmas thing is fake. Is this some sort of adult conspiracy to mislead the children of the world?" and, "The next thing you'll be telling us is that there is no Easter Bunny or Tooth Fairy!"

Dee Ann and I hung our heads at this last statement. Recognizing this gesture as a confirmation of the last statement, the wailing gets louder. They now realize that not only is Christmas done for, but also they will never ever get another Easter egg or find another dollar bill under their pillow. Horror is heaped upon horror.

I looked at Ethan and asked what made him ask the question. At this point Tabitha chimed in: "It's all my fault. After you put us to bed, I sneaked back into Ethan's room and got into the bottom bunk. He asked if I thought that there was a Santa and I said, 'No!' We argued for a while until finally Ethan said he would go and ask Mommy. Daddy," she said, "I really wanted to believe that there was a Santa but all the kids at school said that it was not true!"

I looked at Dee Ann, and she said: "Ethan came down the stairs with a resolute look on his face demanding to know if there really was a Santa Claus. I asked if he really, really, really wanted to know, and he said YES, so I said there is no Santa Claus!"

The final straw came when Ethan made one last statement: "If there is no Santa or Easter Bunny or Tooth Fairy, what else have you lied about? Are you going to tell us there is no God?"

Was this some heat stroke nightmare from Jacuzzi hell? If it was, then how would I make my way back to that "Special place" where we were all happy, rosy cheeked, and ready for Santa to come.

I began my climb back from this surreal scene by throwing out the age-old comebacks used on me as a child. The classics came forth, like: "But kids, nothing has changed. Santa will still come tonight." And, "You are part of a special group now that has to keep this special fairy tale alive for the little children around you!"

Nothing appeals to a conspiracy theorist's vanity more than the possibility that he could be in on the conspiracy. The tears stopped. The wailing ceased. What was once perceived to be a horrific trick played out on the fabric of their lives now became a game in which they were real players. They were no longer pawns. A look of intense satisfaction came over their faces and the questions began to flow: "Can we help with putting out the Christmas gifts?" and, "We need to be careful around the little kids at church because they don't know, do they?" and, "If we're still going to get presents, nothing has really changed. Has it, Dad?"

Something had changed. That evening our children had passed from accepting innocent children into co-conspirators in one of the oldest stories known to our society.

As they made their way back to bed, secure in their newfound knowledge, Dee Ann and I again took time to sit and relax. After a few moments of silence, she said: "I think that went well, didn't it?"

I hit her with a couch pillow.

So what have I learned from this experience?

1. Never, ever, ever leave your wife alone and hyped up on Cocoa on Christmas Eve.

2. Kids are smart and can recognize a cover-up when they see one.

3. Never, ever, ever, tell a child that there is no Santa. Deny, deny and deny again any question of his non-existence.

4. Hot tubs will never be the same for me again.

5. Timing is everything. Wait until your kids are married to set reality straight.

Life Lesson Number 297

—

"Thar She Blows!"

We were visiting my parents in Sydney prior to the Olympics in the year 2000. While we were there, my mother, bless her heart, struck upon the idea that all the boys (both sons and son-in-law) should be treated to a day of white water rafting at the new Olympic white water facility at Penrith. The facility had just opened and was offering anyone who dared (for A$50) the possibility of fame and fortune by allowing him to ride the Olympic course not once, but seven times.

Seven times! That had to be a good deal at any price. Not only would we get the chance to say that we survived the Olympic course, but we could commentate the actual events at the real Olympics from the safety of our armchairs anywhere in the world, thus sharing our wondrous experiences with our closest friends. This was going to be great. This once-in-a-lifetime event was so great that my ten-year-old daughter begged me to allow her to ride the rapids with me. After all, it would be a bonding experience that she would never forget.

I had never experienced a closed whitewater course before. It was an engineering miracle. The start of the course was on the upper part of a hill where a large pool was fed by huge pumps. The course curved down and around to the left, covering about a quarter of a mile and giving the user about ten different rapids to experience. At the bottom of the run, another pool collected the run-off and allowed the participants to load up, practice and/or row over to a large conveyor belt that carried you to the top of the hill. This conveyor then dumped you into the upper pool without your even having to get out of your raft or kayak. Wow, how much effort could this be? I didn't even have to walk to the top of the hill to make the run. They were going to carry me there.

I should have known that things were not going to go smoothly when they called our group's name and then issued us with wet suits, wind-breakers (oh, by the way, this is June in the southern hemisphere...you know...winter), helmets and life jackets. As the group raced to collect comfortably fitting gear, I realized that I had hung back a little too far. By the time I got to the front to get my gear, the assistant looked me up and down (extra, extra, extra large, remember) and said, "Look mate, we might have a bit of a problem with you. You're a bit on the big side, eh?" Never one to miss an opportunity to poke fun at myself, I responded, "So, you're out of "ORCA suits" are ya!" The skinny little fellow responded without even smiling, "Yeah, but try this large one on; you should be able to squeeze into it with a bit a work." Along with the wet suit, he threw me a large windbreaker, helmet and life jacket. I grabbed my old sneakers and wandered off.

Never one who avoids a challenge, I walked out to the lower pool ramp where everyone else was easily throwing on his or her gear. I had on a T-shirt and swimmers and proceeded to lay the gear out on the ground around me. The first to go on was the wet suit. Sure, it was at least two sizes too small, but it was made of rubber and rubber stretches. When it comes to wet suits the legs are always the easy part. They make you feel like you're on a winning streak. With both legs in, you reach down and begin the arduous task of getting the body of the suit up over the rear end and back and then over your shoulders. At this point the going got tough. I managed to get the suit over my shoulders but could not seem to comfortably accommodate my ample girth within the tight confines of the suit.

I could not complain. I dared not ask for help. I just lay down and started rolling around trying to get the zippers closed. I huffed and puffed, sucked in and blew out, all to no avail. Finally, my brother came over and offered to put me out of my misery. He said I looked like a Christmas Beetle on its back in the throes of death. With one deft movement, he placed his foot on my stomach, pushed down, grabbed the zipper and whipped it up over my chest.

I don't know if you have ever seen 350 pounds of flour in a 200 lb sack, but it is not a pretty sight. The rubber was stretched so tight that certain movements caused excruciating pains in certain sensitive areas of my body. One dress item down and only four to go. I sheepishly thanked my brother. I really needed help getting my sneakers on. Goodness knows the wet suit could not handle the breaking strain of me bending over to slide them onto my shapely black pegs. I contorted and convulsed until I managed to slip them on over my lily-white feet. The windbreaker fit fairly well now; it went easily on over the wet suit (since most of the sausage was already stuffed into the casing). I threw on the life jacket, cinched it tightly around me and tried to put on the skullcap helmet.

The final indignity of the process set in. The helmet sat on my great huge size eight-and-a-half-hat-size head like a pimple on a pumpkin. It was the largest helmet that they had. It would have to do. The dressing process was finally finished.

I was ready. I was totally and thoroughly exhausted. My daughter, brother and brother-in-law would just look at me, turn their heads away and laugh. Shame was my friend by this point.

Our boat guide had our group hop into the boat (a task easily accomplished by those physically fit and eager participants with loose-fitting gear.) I, on the other hand, wallowed at the side of the boat, unable to raise my legs up and over the side of the boat lest circulation be cut off to my lower extremities. Finally, I was assisted over the side and into the boat, allowing the training to begin.

Anyone who has ever white-water-rafted goes through a simple training program. At this command you row backward. At this command you row forward. At this command one side rows backward while the other side rows forward. Pretty simple stuff for a group of coordinated people, but this was no group of coordinated people. In all my discomfort, I found myself surrounded by people who could not tell left from right or forward from backward. The guide gave up, declared our training over, and had us set off for the up ramp. This would be fun.

I had stationed myself at the middle of the boat, not really by choice because it was where I fell when I was dragged into the raft. My daughter, slightly frightened now, sat to my right with little tears in her eyes. She was now regretting the thought of even trying this new form of entertainment. I looked at her with loving Daddy eyes and said, "Don't worry, Tabby, everything will be all right. You're going to love this!" I lied of course. I had an ominous feeling that all would not be well. I feared for my daughter's life as well as my own. I feigned machismo and high-fived my brother and brother-in-law. My little Tabitha began to settle down.

The first trip down the rapids was very straightforward. The course was meticulously designed so that a crane could pick up boulders and blocks to change the flow and severity of the course. These boulders would pass harmlessly under the boat if we completed all ten rapids without incident. I looked at my daughter. She was hooked for life. The thrill of the run had reddened her cheeks and she wanted to move forward a position so she could be closer to the front where the action was.

We made our way back to the conveyor ramp and began the process again. The water was cold, the wind quite intense and my lower back was really starting to hurt. On the second run I noticed that the designers had landscaped pedestrian walkways around the outside of the run. This allowed family, friends and photographers to wander around and watch their loved ones as they risked their lives at each rapid. Positioned at each rapid was an employee of the Olympic course. This person held a throw bag filled with rescue rope. If things went poorly and you fell out of the boat, he would throw the bag to you, and you would grab it and hold on to the rope as he pulled you to the side. Once at the side, you could safely get out of the raging torrents and walk back to the bottom of the hill.

As normally happens with a group of testosterone-enhanced males, the majority of the group wanted the boat guide to be more daring on each circuit of the course. The guide, of course, obliged. He had us backing down rapids, spinning around, and generally acting the fool with our lives. All the while, my daughter kept edging towards the front, taking on more risk and loving every minute.

Things came apart for me on run number five (of seven) and rapid number four (of ten). The guide had determined that the only way to soothe the savage daredevil masses in our raft was to "surf" the bottom of rapid number four. I must admit that I did not protest too much at this "surfing" because, after all, if Tabitha could do it, so could Daddy. Surfing entailed turning the raft sideways in the wake at the bottom of the rapid and sliding up and down the runoff wake without moving on to the next rapid. We watched other groups do this and they appeared to be having lots of fun. No one fell into the raging waters. No one drowned.

It was our turn now. We positioned ourselves off to the side of rapid four and made our way into the wake. Our boat slid up and down the wake of the rapid. All was well. We were having fun. The raft was acting like a large surfboard with nine people on it. Then my large brother-in-law lost his balance, leaned back, and knocked me out of the raft on the side closest to the rapid. I tried not to panic. I had fallen into rapids before. I held my breath and threw up my arms, and what do I feel? The bottom of the raft above me. Thank goodness the rushing water pushed my large carcass out from under the raft. As direct during the training session, I looked up and watched as the lifeguard on the bank threw the rope bag into the air directly at me.

It was a beautiful arc, straight and true to my waiting arms. I grabbed the bag with all my might and looked back at my little life savior on the bank. Bystanders would later confirm the fiasco that occurred. This mighty little one hundred and fifty pound lifesaver had hooked him a big one. He leaned back on the rope struggling to get a purchase with the heels of his boots. In his small mind he figured that if he dug in, the current would turn his catch to the side where it could climb out to safety. In actuality, the poor little fellow began what one viewer described as "the best darn ground plowing I have ever seen with two heels. Two furrows straight, deep and true." Another viewer posited, "If ever there is an Olympic event for grass skiing, you two should enter!"

From my perspective, all I could see were two wide eyes as the lifesaver shot across the grass like a water-skier. He was obviously too frightened or stunned to let go of the rope. It was either "me or him," I thought. I could hold on and drag this little fellow to his death or let go and ride these waves down six more rapids to the bottom. How bad could that be? So I let go. In the few moments I had before rapid five was upon me, I did get a glimpse of the look of relief on the life-saver's face as I threw my arms back, freeing him from certain death by dragging. I turned to face downstream, steeled myself for the onslaught and prepared to ride all the way to the bottom.

Rapid five hit me like a steel hammer in my chest. As I surged over the rapid and down into the wake my rear end met with some of the obstacles so lovingly placed below the surface to create the maelstrom above. I did surface, which is a good thing when you like to breathe. I managed to get in about half a breath before rapid six hit me.

Now rapid six was no worse than rapid five but one problem began to emerge that began to cause me great discomfort. At each rapid pounding I realized that I was slipping further and further down through my floatation jacket so that all that was visible from the bank was a life jacket with no head, just an empty skull-cap bobbing along.

By rapid seven I told myself that I was in serious trouble. No use fighting it. Air was a luxury for me, but at least I was occasionally getting a whiff between waves. Rapids eight and nine found me telling myself that death was inevitable. I was now severely oxygen deprived and choking on water in my throat. I was so weak I could not hold my legs up in a crouching position to avoid the boulders under the water. I crashed into them unmercifully. Could I make it one more rapid? What choice did I have?

At the bottom of rapid ten the water became calm. My seemingly lifeless body floated like a dead puffer fish on the top of the slowing waters. With what strength I had left, I reached out and grabbed a wire mesh that made up one of the retaining walls on the side of the bottom pool. Opening my eyes I saw for the first time in my life what I thought was my dead grandfather beckoning me to go with him. He was reaching down and trying to take my hand. I released the wire to grab him, but the swirling waters carried me away to a little rock beach where I beached like a sick pilot whale.

People floated by in their boats. Some looked on in amusement. Some even asked if I were okay. I could not talk. I could not move. I just lay there bobbing up and down on the rocks, rolling backwards and forwards with the waves.

Sometime during this floating period, I was able to look up and see my daughter standing up in the front of the raft shouting at me. She was laughing and saying, "That was cool Dad, and can you do it again?" I declined with a tired wave of my hand, beckoning them to continue the journey without me. I again slipped into an exhausted haze, floating, bobbing, and wafting up against the rocks.

As oxygen began to make it back to my extremities, I began to stir. I managed to get up on one elbow and view this horrid course for the last time. Just then I looked up and saw a small blonde girl on rapid six, standing in the front of the raft, holding on to the bow rope, riding the raft down the rapids. I swear she was yelling, "Yeha!" as she rode the boat like a wild bronco all the way to the bottom. I started to think to myself, "What sort of idiot would want to do that!" As the young girl approached me at the shoreline, the first words out of her mouth were, "Dad. We have to do this again!"

We had survived. I was battered and bruised. I had fallen and was almost ready to get up. At least I had my dignity. As I wallowed at the rocky shoreline, the members of my crew unloaded, gave me a nod and made their way to the change rooms to go home. I felt pretty good about the whole thing (having survived) until the last one in passing said, "Nice wetsuit. You might want to try wearing the right side out next time!"

So what have I learned from this experience?

1. You can never underestimate the fearless energy of an excited ten-year-old girl.

2. Time certainly does change your perspective on what constitutes fun.

3. You can't get three hundred and fifty pounds of flour in a two hundred pound bag. (Well, you actually can, but it ain't pretty.)

4. Never let testosterone make decisions for you.

5. Oxygen is a good thing. Use it wisely and never sparingly.

6. Mass and acceleration can overcome inertia in the blink of an eye.

7. If you watch the kayak broadcast from the Olympic white water rafting circuit and you look really closely at rapid five you can actually see two shoe width plough marks leading down to the water's edge.

Life Lesson Number 300

—

"Who let the cat out of the bag?"

There was no doubt about it: the cat and I did not like each other. Things had gone downhill between us since the cat-shaving incident. Of course, the constant strain of living with three dufus dogs (that found it hard to tell the difference between "a cat" and "the cat"), and two rambunctious kids (that paid this poor little kitty way too much "attention"), and let's not forget the cat-shaving freak would make any cat a little testy, to say the least.

Why did I not like the cat? The cat had continued its annoying habits of sitting on my face and shocking me awake during the night, and let's not forget the special messages that I might find in our closets. I had had enough.

In recent weeks I had resorted to psychological operations to gain the upper hand in the situation. I had started letting the dogs into the house just to annoy the cat. The cat of course would seek high ground on a table or breakfast bar and stand nervously watching the dogs run around. The level of tension in the cat was noticeable. His fur would stand up and he could not relax until the dogs left.

When I got tired of the dogs in the house, I would open the back door and let them go outside. After a few minutes of trembling on top of the breakfast bar, the cat would noticeably settle down, relax, and slump into a ball to "get over" the trauma of what had just happened. You could actually see the tension roll out of his furry little body. This was my opportunity.

The moment the cat let its guard down, I would walk to the other side of the room behind where the cat was sitting, and throw a cushion at the counter. When the cushion hit, the cat would shoot up at least three feet into the air thinking that a dog had been left behind. I would laugh; the cat would land, turn, and look at me and then slink off. I know you think I am terrible, but don't feel sorry for that cat. He would get his own back at me at night by springing on my groin area as I slept. It was a running battle that neither of us could win.

Things finally progressed to the point where I shut the bedroom door to keep the cat out. Up until now we had worried about the small children and had left our door open, but the cat antics put an end to that.

Early one morning I awoke before the alarm. I don't usually do that, but I found that I needed to go and get a drink of water from the kitchen. As I opened the door, I noticed something on the floor. It was white and about three feet long. It had not been there the night before when I went to bed. I had no idea what it was. Bending over to get a closer look I noticed that one end of the white object appeared to be a crouching white cat while the other end appeared to be an inflated four inch by twelve inch long white plastic food bag. How confusing!

Without even thinking I reached down, grabbed the plastic bag and pulled. As it separated from the cat's head, the cat took several deep breaths, looked up at me and staggered drunkenly down the hallway.

Now, I know that you will think that I am terrible, but I actually made the Homer Simpson "Doh" sound as I realized how close we had just been to being "a cat free zone." "Five more minutes," I said out loud to myself. "I couldn't have slept for five more minutes!" I had let the cat out of the bag. I went back to bed dejected.

From this day forward the cat was never the same. I suspect that he suffered some brain damage through lack of oxygen. He went from being an annoying cat to being Attila the cat. His reign of terror grew to the point that he ruled the house; the kids ran from him; the dogs feared him; my wife barely tolerated him, and I left him alone.

So what have I learned from this experience?

1. In a war of nerves a cat will always win.

2. Cover your garbage or put it out before going to bed.

3. It's amazing what a difference five minutes can make in your life.

4. Is there a cat CPR course that owners can take?

5. Fear the fractious cat!

6. Cats are patient.

7. Cats know where you sleep.

8. Cats rule the night.

9. Remember, you eventually have to go to sleep.

10. If you like your cat, you should never leave plastic food bags in your garbage.

11. Sometimes you regret letting the cat out of the bag.

12. There is only one thing worse than an annoying cat, and that's a "crazy annoying cat."

Life Lesson Number 302

—

"The very bad day!"

August 8th, 2000. My very bad day...

Score: Daddy—1 : Cats—0

To understand the events of the past few days, and the flow of this story, you have to know the following joke.

◆　　　　◆　　　　◆

A homeowner wants to go on holidays and needs to leave someone in charge of his precious cat. He gets his neighbor (Fred) to take care of the cat, leaving detailed instructions on what to give him, how he needs to be treated and how special the cat is. This is the first time that the homeowners' have been separated from the cat, so they were really hesitant to leave the cat with someone else. The volunteer neighbor (Fred) tells them not to worry, he has their contact numbers and address for the hotel, and he says that he will contact them if something happens.

The cat family leaves on vacation and checks into their hotel.

On day two of the vacation, the cat escaped from the house when Fred went to the door, it climbed a tree and then jumped to the top of the house. The neighbor can't get up there, so he throws stones at the cat hoping to encourage it to come down. One of these stones hits the cat, knocking it to the ground dead.

Fred is quite perplexed. What should he do? He decides that the best way to handle this is to tell the owners quickly. But, he could not bring himself to actually speak to them about it. So Fred sends a telegram to the hotel:

"Cat Dead Love Fred"

Well, of course, the owners were horrified. They called Fred immediately and lamented both the death of the cat and the method of message delivery. The owner said, "Fred, you don't just say, 'Cat dead love Fred.' You have to break bad news to people gently. If you have to break bad news, spread it out a little. Tell us over a period of time."

Fred asked how that should be done, and the owners suggested the following.

Telegram 1: "Cat is on the roof and won't come down…"
Telegram 2: "Cat has had a terrible fall, taken to hospital…"
Telegram 3: "Cat on life support, not expected to live…"
Telegram 4: "Cat passed quietly into the afterlife…no pain"

"Now that is how you tell someone that their precious loved one has passed away," the owner said.

Well, time passes as it does in all jokes. The neighbor never did get another cat because his mother-in-law had moved in with them. It came time again for the neighbor to go on vacation. He asks Fred to watch over the house and mother-in-law just to make sure everything would be okay. Fred said that he would.

Sure enough, two days into their vacation the neighbors receive a telegram.

"Mother-in-law is on the roof and won't come down!"

◆   ◆   ◆

So now I can relate to you this story of my "Very bad day" and how it started.

Saturday 8:00 AM

- Oreo (the cat) was in a particularly bad mood. He hisses at our visitors and tries to bite them as I carry him from the bedroom where he was locked overnight (lest he eat our sister-in-law's baby). I felt better now that the cat was locked in the laundry. He could do little physical damage there.

Monday 8:00 AM

- With the cat subdued, we made it through to Monday without incident. Our visitors left. What a relief!

"Oreo on roof and won't come down."

Monday 8:15 AM

- Oreo goes to vet for shot.
- Bites vet and scratches up Dee Ann and Tabitha.
- Vet fee $55.

"Oreo has horrible fall from roof. Severely injured."

Monday 5:40 PM

- Oreo is hissing at kids at the front door and biting Tabitha.

"Oreo taken to hospital in dire condition"

Tuesday 6:40 AM

- Oreo bites Tabitha as we take him to be groomed.

"Oreo on life support...outcome not looking good"

Tuesday 12:00 PM

- Phone call from the groomer with the message that they could not handle the cat.
- Oreo had attacked two associates and it had taken three people to get him into cage.
- These people were not happy with Oreo since blood had been let.

"Oreo near death"

Tuesday 1:00 PM

- Daddy drops by to pick up Oreo from the groomers, opens the cage and reaches in, Oreo latches on to the thumb of the hand that feeds him (bad move on his part as he would find out later).

Tuesday 1:05 PM

- Arterial blood squirting from thumb.
- Daddy quietly closes cage with the Ors (as Tabitha sometimes called him) still in it, grabs thumb, tries to staunch bleeding for twenty minutes.

Tuesday 1:25 PM

- Blood flow finally ceases (tourniquet sought but not required).
- Groomers tell me to take cage and cat and get out of Dodge...

"Oreo on life support, not looking good"

Tuesday 1:30 PM

- Oreo trying to bite me through cage as I drive off.

Tuesday 1:31 PM

- Call Mommy and advise that I am on my way to the Vet to have Ors join that Asian Youth league (Euthanasia).
- She concurs based on goings-on this last week.

"Oreo on life support—do not resuscitate order (DNR) given"

Tuesday 1:45 PM

- Drop Oreo by vet.
- Vet not there.
- Leave carrier (since we couldn't get him out), sign DNR papers, and leave to await the vet's call before the plug is pulled.

Tuesday 2:00 PM

- Family council at the house.
- Tabitha understood why and concurred, through many tears and cuddles that he needed to go to the big cat hunting ground in the sky.

Tuesday 2:01 PM to 3:00 PM

- Ethan storming around house trying to find the phone number of the vet so as to stop this unjust killing.
- Ethan calls parents murderers.
- Ethan states that there was nothing wrong with the cat (even though it scared him to death and he would not pick it up).

- After holding Ethan in cuddle huddle for forty minutes, he settles down to the point that we can talk.
- All family crying, saying that he was our cat as well and that we all loved him and that this was the best for him, since we could not send him to another house the way he was acting.
- Things settle temporarily.

Tuesday 4:00 PM

- Vet calls and talks to Mommy to ask about situation prior to pulling plug.
- Mommy gives the past history of bites and attacks as well as the last three days of problems.
- Vet says she does not usually put animals to sleep unless there are extenuating circumstances.
- Vet called Oreo a Fractious cat.
- These are cats that have split personalities. Loving one minute—violent the next.
- Vet concurred that it was in our best interest (lest we replace the phrase "a dingo got my baby" with "Oreo got my baby") that he take the big dirt nap.
- Ethan hears only the part that he is a normal cat part of the time and runs off screaming about murder again.

Tuesday 4:05 PM

- Told the vet that we will pick up the dead Oreo for last rites and interment at the house after the plug had been pulled.

Tuesday 4:10 PM

- Vet still trying to get fractious Oreo out of cage.

Tuesday 4:15 PM

- Muscle relaxant given to settle him down (don't know how they did this, but they may have used a blow gun with that blue frog dart poison).

Tuesday 4:30 PM

- Plug pulled on life support. No pain.
- It takes another thirty minutes to get the message through to Ethan that the Vet said we're doing the right thing.

"Oreo dead, love Fred"

Tuesday 4:45 PM

- Assassin father sent to pick up cardboard box and pay $55.00 to vet for membership in the Asian Youth league (ouch—two days in a row).
- No offer by Vet to refund yesterday's shots (surprise).

Tuesday 5:00 PM

- 98 degrees and 100 percent humidity.
- Oreo delivered to my car in a large UPS box two feet by two feet (he's big…but not that big).
- This reminds me of the dead draft horse story my Dad told (Class Title: How to bury a draft horse—101, requirements: shovel, pick, half size hole and an axe…).
- I look at the box and decide that I need a smaller box or I will be digging until well after midnight.

Tuesday 5:10 PM

- Locate smaller box.
- Decide to cut it down even further and make the transfer of 14-pound package to the new smaller box and duct tape it shut.
- It was a little tight—but hey, comfort was the least of my worries.

Tuesday 5:30 PM

- Interment location found at front of house in landscaping (where Oreo used to roll around in the mulch according to Tabitha, his favorite spot).

Tuesday 5:45 PM

- Digging.
- Daddy first.

Tuesday 6:00 PM

- Digging.
- Ethan next (extreme interest in interment of said feline).
- Requested that he also be a pallbearer for the said box.
- Tabitha agrees.

Tuesday 6:15 PM

- Digging and much sweating.
- Tabitha sitting on lawn holding box, tears running down face quietly, mourning the loss of her first cat.

Tuesday 6:30 PM

- Services held on front lawn.
- Tabitha and Ethan carry box together to grave and place him in the ground (lips quivering).
- Daddy gets the dirty look from Ethan (I can see this coming out in therapy in later years).

Tuesday 6:40 PM

- Hole filling starts with Ethan really getting into it.
- Ethan asking good questions like, "How long before the worms get him?" and "What will he look like when he rots?"
- Good healthy questions that make me think the he will be digging the cat up next month.

Tuesday 6:45 PM

- Visitation begins with kids from neighborhood coming over and getting the whole story.

- Lots of tears, cuddles and dirty looks at Dad.

Tuesday 7:00 PM

- Pizza and video.

- Prayer for pizza involves request to take care of Oreo in cat heaven (while looking at Dad through slit eyes).

Tuesday 9:00 PM

- Kids off to bed making plans to get new cat next Monday when they return from Grandma's house.

All this happened after having spent the first two hours of the day at the doctors' with the worst ear infection in both ears I have ever had. So, how was your day?

So what have I learned from this experience?

1. Never bite the hand that feeds you.

2. Cuddle Huddles are less snuggles and more trouble than they are worth.

3. Even in death, the cat can still stick it to a father.

4. Does the cost of future therapy for my children really offset the emotional cost of the cat's reign of terror?

5. Always keep some blue frog dart poison handy. You never know when you might need it.

Signed,

"The murderer"

Life Lesson Number 324

—

"Fire in the Hole!"

I just wanted to humiliate myself (one more time) by telling you a funny story about what happened to me this weekend. It was one of those situations where you think things can't get any worse, but they do.

Let me set the background picture so you understand how and where this happened.

We have had Vacation Bible School play practice at the church building every evening and every day for the last three weeks. Sunday afternoon was no different. We finished at about 4:00 PM, which gave us just enough time to rush home to my favorite toilet (you know, the one that you're comfortable with) and take care of business, before returning to church. There's no place like home; there's no place like home.

So on arrival I rush into our little bathroom at home, take care of business and sigh that sigh that we all sigh when that sense of great relief comes over us. Now, being the good husband that I am, and under strict instructions from my wife as to toilet etiquette, I reach down for a small decorative glass candle and a book of matches to light the "incense fire."

I balance the small candle on my bare knee, strike the match, light the wick inside the glass and, reaching down, try to place the candle and matchbook on the floor. At this point, the candle slips, flipping on its side. Not a problem; I reach down and flip it back up, trying not to disturb the lovely decorative rope and flower ornaments around the candle. I return to my relaxation, and begin to read.

Problem!

When I had gently set the candle back in the upright position, a small piece of string had accidentally ended up dangling about an inch and half over the candle flame. High enough to not ignite immediately but long enough to lull me into a sense of relaxation. The offending string then proceeds to ignite into a lovely blue flame about three inches high. At this point I now have two open flames in the bathroom (candlewick and string).

Problem!

I scream for help, but no one hears me as the toilet door, bathroom door, and bedroom door are all shut. It is like being in Maxwell Smart's cone of silence. Since I knew that the combination of two open flames in a closed chamber filled with gas is not a good thing, panic begins to set in. Reaching down, I grab the candle jar and bring it close to my face blowing as hard as I can to put out the string fire.

Problem!

Important safety tip. Never, I repeat, never blow on a burning object with your pants down around your ankles. Why? Because small particles of burning debris tend to waft off and float downwards, sending hot coals into your under-wear and onto the (what I perceive to be highly flammable) toilet carpet.

(So, let me give you a visual recap of the situation at this point. I now have fire in the candle, fire on the string, hot coals in my underwear and burning embers on the carpet around the toilet [where I am still sitting]. Things could not get worse.)

Problem!

After much huffing and blowing at the open flame, the burning string finally goes out. At this point a temporary sense of relief overcomes me as a crisis appears to have been averted.

Wrong!

There is still much smoke coming from the burning string and hot embers are still wafting away to do whatever damage they can.

In hindsight, my next move was really questionable.

With the burning ember being so large (and my hands full at that time), the thought crossed my mind that I should lick my fingers and snuff out the burning string. "But," I thought to myself, "you will burn your thumb and finger if you do that." I then made a fateful choice. I said to myself, "Just wad up a huge bundle of toilet paper and grab the wick! The pressure will snuff out the ember since it will be in the middle of the paper and it won't flame up." (Don't go there. I know, I know…)

So I grab the toilet roll, give it one mighty pull, and about six feet of paper hits the floor. I quickly do the lasso movement with my arm, wrapping the paper around my hand. I then crush the toilet paper into a tight ball telling myself that things are starting to look up. I then take the wadded paper, grab the burning string embers and snuff them out. A great sense of relief came over me.

Wrong!

As I snuff out the embers of the string (you know, that string that was right over the burning candle wick which was still alight inside the jar), the outer papers of the large wad of toilet paper catches alight. Now if you have never seen that wafer-thin toilet paper react to an open flame, I would suggest doing a small experiment OUTSIDE. Needless to say, I am now sitting on the porcelain perch, pants down around my ankles, burning candle in my left hand and flaming toilet paper in my right hand. I am now screaming for help and starting to cough from the smoke.

Problem!

At this point I realize I have but one option with the flaming toilet paper. I stand up, trying to keep my unclean nether regions over the porcelain, reach between my legs with a flaming wad of toilet paper and throw it into the bowl. I did this because in my feeble-addled mind the toilet bowl had water in it and water is fire's enemy.

WRONG!

The consistency of wadded toilet paper is such that it is light enough to float. Thus, I find myself straddling a porcelain pyre with flames about 12 inches high.

Problem!

At this point I lose my balance, as I am trying to lean away from the flames (remember that bare behind thing), and fall headfirst towards the door catching myself with my now empty right hand. Being off balance, I pushed back off the closed toilet door, over-corrected ($E=MC$ squared—momentum is a terrible thing), and fell back on the flaming porcelain pyre.

BIG PROBLEM!

Why it took me so long to think about hitting the flusher, I don't know. Perhaps it was the sheer horror of imagining how I would explain this situation to the emergency room doctor, or, worse, how the crime scene investigation team from the coroner's office would write this up without laughing. But I finally did hit the flusher.

In the time it took that burning toilet paper to do two laps of the bowl and disappear, it did the best depilatory job on a hairy bum you have ever seen.

So what have I learned from this experience?

1. Never close more than one door between you and a possible rescue squad.

2. Remove all decorative paraphernalia from a candle before using it under industrial conditions.

3. Never, I repeat, NEVER, assume that wadded paper will snuff out a burning ember.

4. Never put flaming objects between your bare legs.

5. Burning paper floats AND CONTINUES TO BURN.

6. In the time it takes for burning toilet tissue to make two rounds of a toilet bowl, it can do a lot of damage.

Hairlesly yours,

Ian

Life Lesson Number 400

—

"Girth Mirth"

There comes a time in fat peoples' lives when their profound girth starts to present problems. What kinds of problems you might ask. "All sorts," I say to you skinny people out there. "To a skinny person this might be hard to imagine, but it's hard to keep your clothes on when you're fat." A horrible visual, but it is true.

The best way for me to describe this problem is to give those of you who are corpulently challenged a visual example using fruit. Take the common household pear. The shape of "the pear" is such that it is rounded away from a central large circumference that is midway up the height of "the pear." Now if you were to take a rubber band and put it on that large circumference, what happens? That's right: the rubber band rolls either up to the top of "the pear" or down to the base of "the pear." It is practically impossible to keep the rubber band where it should be in "the middle" of "the pear." It would require an engineering miracle that has so far eluded the clothing makers of the world to this day, who, by the way, all work for skinny people.

As a fat man, I have a choice. I can go with the above-the-waist full circumference pant that fights to climb above or drop below the ample girth zone called my waist, or I can go with the low-rider look. This is the look which makes you realize that you are fighting a losing battle with your circumference. And you decide to cinch your pants tightly below your belly line but over your ample bottom cheeks. It is not a good look, but it is often the only practical solution; however, when viewed by a skinny person, it is often referred to as "the overlap."

Let's face it, fat people; we can't fight gravity. I am a fat person; I have been struggling with suspenders, belts, elastic waists and every other form of clothing suspension for years. None of it works well. You've all seen some of the moves that we fat guys have. You know the "jolly roll" in which you laugh and cinch up your pants and tuck in your shirt to get the pants back to where they belong, or the "wallet check" which looks s if you're checking your wallet, but you're actually pulling up your underpants that have slipped down to your knees. Oh the joy!

My father chose the low rider look. I tried it for a while, but it just didn't work for me. I went with the full circumference pant and have been paying the price ever since. Just the other day I walked into our garage and reached above my head to grab something. The act of reaching up caused a slight slimming effect. (I know: I thought about it, but you can't walk around with your hands above your head all day.) As I grabbed for the object above me, my pants fell effortlessly to the floor. They did not touch a thing. It was a sheer, clear, free fall from my waist to the ground. Now you can see how my pear analogy works here, can't you? Thank goodness that the garage door was open and only three or four cars were driving by. I could have been really embarrassed.

The worst thing that can happen to a fat person occurs when he has both hands full. You know, when you're carrying stuff in from the car or helping someone in the office and then, oh my, what do you say in situations like that when you're holding the bags and your suit pants are buffing the linoleum? "I do have underwear on, don't I? Phew what a relief!" or "Hello! Bet you weren't expecting that to happen! Neither was I!" There is a reason that we fat people are jovial and good-natured. We have to be just to get through the day.

Now some of you are saying: "What about suspenders. Surely they are the solution to your dilemma!" I say "Solution, no, torture devices, YES!"

Let me ask you this: how many fat people have you seen that look comfortable while wearing suspenders? The answer is none! Let's get real here. They are devices that were designed to punish the corpulent population by creating the rare "north of the equator" effect that you rarely hear fat people talk about. The "north of the equator" effect is the high ride up of the suspendered pants as they break free of the large circumference and race upwards towards the North Pole.

This condition is typified by the Tweedle Dee and Tweedle Dum look and is accompanied by an uncomfortable walking gate that is typified by the male's inability to "dress" either left or right comfortably. In my estimation, suspenders are probably the prime cause of infertility in fat males. So, suspenders are out for me.

I have thought about this for a long time and I think I might have a solution. Will somebody please come out with a "Shant?" It will be the saving grace for fat people. In my corpulent dreams, a shant is a shirt/pant jump suit for fat people that looks like two different garments but is joined in the middle; no ride up and no ride down. One can only hope, but I am not holding my breath for someone

to make it because—"oops!" There they go again "I do have underwear on, don't
I?"

So what have I learned from this experience?

1. Gravity sucks.

2. You should never make fat people carry stuff.

3. The next time you eat a pear, I know what you will be thinking!

4. I am thinking about having snaps sewn to my waist and fitted to my under-
    wear.

5. Fat people should always wear clean underwear and nice socks.

6. Long-tailed shirts also help in embarrassing situations.

7. Perhaps a naked fat person protest might encourage the fashion world to
    address our little problem.

8. The next time my pants drop to the floor, I'm stepping out and moving on
    without them.

Life Lesson Number 463

—

"The Mountain Romance!"

When my wife suggested a romantic getaway with a group of friends, I thought to myself "that would be nice." She said that we were going to walk to a chalet on top of a mountain, eat a romantic dinner, and then walk back down the mountain the next day. At the time, it did not strike me that actual effort would be involved in "walking" to the top of the mountain.

I am a large man. How large you might ask? Just let me say that my girth is somewhat "awesome in its profundity." To put the effort of this walk into perspective, it is like asking a 250 pound out-of-condition linebacker to carry two fifty pound bags of flour eight miles straight up a mountain. Now picture this: I get out of breath moving my chair between the desk and the computer in my office. In my naiveté, I figured that just walking wouldn't hurt me. After all, how hard could it be?

There were twelve in our group, all friends, anxious to get going and reveling in the camaraderie of this shared experience. Several of the group had made the trek the previous year and were champing at the bit to get to the top again.

I should have known how bad things were going to be. During the night before we left to walk up the mountain, a large storm front moved through the area. The temperature dropped into the low sixties and the rain was falling heavily. Needless to say, like the good trooper that I am, I donned my hiking clothes, threw on my backpack, draped a rain poncho over everything and set out up the side of the mountain.

Monday

Hour 1

I knew that I would slow the group down, so my wife and I set off ahead of everyone else enjoying the misty mountainside, the lush vegetation, and the exhilaration of this experience together. At first we stopped occasionally and took pictures of each other. After about twenty minutes the group caught up to us. The rain was bearable. The cool crispness of the day made walking seem almost fun.

Sometime during this first hour, two things happened: my feet and shoes got wet, and a competitive nature emerged in the group as to who would get to the top first. Needless to say, the competitive group members quickly abandoned the slower members of the group faster than terrorists abandoning their training camps this last week. So much for the group experience.

Life was still good. I could still smile. But my feet were wet and starting to hurt.

Hour 2

In the second hour the stark realization set in that we had seven hours to go and that I was about to die. I knew I was about to die because with each breath my chest burned. Not only that, but the burn in my legs and back was almost unbearable. The further I go, the slower I get, finally ending up at the back of the slow-moving pack.

At this point, the first unpleasant thoughts begin to bounce around inside my head about those who organized this romantic getaway. Simple things like, "I'm going to give them a piece of my mind when I see them." Nothing too dramatic—after all, I consider myself a good and kind man, one who is tolerant of others and their faults and never, I repeat, never given to thoughts of harming anyone.

Hour 3

I can barely move. Each step is a new and most unpleasant agony. I find myself wondering where the sherpas are and shouldn't they be here by now with my oxygen bottles. I am now, in my fevered oxygen deprived addled mind, wishing that the trip organizer would stumble and perhaps break a toe or perhaps even sprain an ankle. Any minor injury to slow the group down and to divert them from this diabolical mountain quest that they have thrust upon us. It is not too late to turn around and drag ourselves back down this horrid mountain. If we turned now, we could at least escape with our dignity intact, having succumbed to the elements and horrors of the climb.

Hour 4

We have reached the point of no return. I am devastated by this realization. If we turned around now we would probably be found frozen in the morning by some hyperactive scout troop on bivouac. My hallucinations continue. I have never hit anyone out of spite in my life and now was not the time to start. But I began to reason that I could hire someone to smack the leader of the group for me. I would not be doing the smacking myself, I reasoned. I had a workable plan.

At this point I looked down at my feet and saw two overstuffed kielbasa sausages bulging out of my sneakers and socks. "This is not good," I thought to myself. If my ankles and legs swell any bigger, I may need medical assistance to remove my shoes. Then my oxygen-deprived brain thought "perhaps I can turn this medical disaster into some advantage for myself." I begin to point out to the group the great huge swelling, preparing them for what I saw as my inevitable collapse and their sisyphusian task of carrying me the rest of the way up the mountain on their backs. I now had another plan.

Hour 5

The sciatic nerves in both my legs were being plucked like fresh chickens in a Pot Pie factory. Each and every step now sent jolting electrical shots up my back and down to my ankles. At a break in the climb, I lay on the ground gasping for air and fumbled for my cell phone. It was out of range. I was unable to arrange for either a hit man or a good divorce lawyer. At this point in the trip, my rings disappeared into my swollen hands. I tried to make a fist but couldn't. I couldn't punch anyone if I tried.

Hour 6

We had reached a point on this precipitous climb where the trail skirted a sheer drop. I was not told of this before I had trekked six miles up a mountain to a place where I would surely have refused to cross under normal conditions. There was a ledge about two feet wide and thirty feet long that slid off down the side of the mountain. It had a wire guide bolted into the side of the mountain for the less fleet of foot.

I froze. I took stock of the situation. My swollen feet and hands had completely refused any mental request to act normally for the last hour. My oxygen-deprived brain was given to moments of imbalance, thus causing me to stagger drunkenly out of control. What was it that gave me the hope that would allow me get to the other side of this suicidal drop? Was it the thought that I would freeze to death where I stood? Was it the thought of my fatherless children crying over the freshly closed grave of their father? No, it was the thought of catching up to the person who organized this Changi Death march and wringing her neck! Up until this point in my life vengeance had never been a motivating factor. But I figured that the organizer had brought me here to kill me. The organizers would get what they deserved.

Hour 7

My darkest hour began with the final climb to the summit. Each and every step was accompanied by bouts of nausea, dizziness and vertigo. I would take five steps and have to stop to get my breath. I spent a significant amount of time in this section of the trail trying to figure out how to get airlifted by medical chopper to the relative warmth and safety of a hospital. I could not go on. I had reached the limit of my endurance.

It was then that it happened. I fell back on my pack, looked longingly at my wife, and said, "Kill me now and use my body for food." She thought I was joking, but I was ready to go.

Hour 8

The eighth hour of the day found us at the peak of the mountain. All that was left was a one-mile hike down to the chalet. The others set off, leaving me alone and dejected. My wife went on ahead a few hundred feet leaving me to myself. It was at this point that my dead grandfather came to me. He was beckoning me to come towards the light and I really wanted to go. I could not feel my left arm, my jaw ached, I was swollen to twice my normal size (and that was huge). I was sure that I was in congestive heart failure and Gramps was here to lead me home. I staggered on towards him, inwardly smiling because now it would all soon be over. Then something distracted me. It was another voice calling me in another direction. It was my wife standing at the entrance to the chalet. She asked me where I thought I was going. I told her, "I am going to heaven to be with Gramps." She said, "No you're not, you'll be late for dinner." So I turned from the release of death and did as my loving wife had asked me.

Hour 9

There isn't enough rust in the word rustic to describe the conditions at the chalet. It would best be described as an abandoned logging camp that even little furry animals shun. The decor was "Prehistoric Hewn." Lanterns for lighting, buckets of warm water for bathing, and a "one holer" to satisfy the potty-trained masses. The cabins had three smaller rooms off a small central log room. Each room had a hewn double bunk double bed. I collapsed onto the bottom bunk, hitting my head. I remained there for an hour, until the feeling in my left arm and jaw came back to normal. The rustic beauty of the camp was only enhanced by the driving wind and rain that whipped in through the cracks.

Hour 10

Dinner is served. I stumble down to the dinning room. I find it filled with merry campers. I immediately decide that I hate them all. The food was plentiful if not good, but I cannot eat. All I can see is the death march in reverse on the morrow.

Tuesday

Hour 1

I had slept fitfully throughout the night. I was too ill to eat breakfast and could barely down a cup of coffee. After all, today was the day that I was going to die. Or at least that is what I thought.

Once again, Dee Ann and I set off first. We knew that the others would catch up to us and we did not want to give them the opportunity of avoiding our dead lifeless bodies draped dramatically in horrific poses. We wanted them to feel true guilt at having subjected us to these conditions. They would have to bear our lifeless corpses to the bottom of the mountain. This would be a suitable punishment for them.

The weather conditions had worsened during the night. We set off in thirty mile an hour wind and forty-degree Fahrenheit temperatures. I am near tears at the hopelessness of our situation. There was one consolation: the ice covering on the fir trees around us looked like a beautiful death shroud. We began with an uphill section. I took one step at a time until we finally reached the top of the mountain again. I looked around and checked for my dead Gramps, but it was obviously too cold for him to be out.

We made pretty good time downhill to the section of the trail with the guide wire. Clouds mercifully covered the sheer drop. Dee Ann and I had talked about comfort zones and how people need to deal with their fears. At this point I am out of my comfort zone, into my stretch zone, and verging on sheer terror.

As I face the wire, my wife consoles me with passages of encouragement like, "You are a sure footed lama" and, "You are a wooly mammoth impervious to the dangers that surround you." Not really King David's Song of Solomon material but close enough to talk me across the death trap.

I make it across and I dance the "Rocky dance" while yelling the theme of Rocky. My spirits rise. I am not dead and it's all downhill from here.

Hour 2

Things are looking up. We are making good time and I am impervious to the snow and ice falling around me. I am now on a quest. A quest for "The Car." Like an old horse turned for home, I begin to bolt downhill almost laughing joyously at the ease with which each step is taken. That is, at least until my knee started to hurt. I now see that even the mountain has a sense of vengeance. It wanted to kill me going both ways.

Hour 3

It was sometime during the third hour of our downhill stint that the temperature dropped to below forty degrees. Accompany that temperature with a wind of thirty miles an hour and you get conditions conducive to hypothermia. I noticed that ice was forming on the hair of my arms. I was starting to shiver. Things could not get much worse, I thought to myself. But then it happened. I ruptured a hemorrhoid. Now like any good engine that blows a gasket, I was faced with the choice of driving on and risking severe damage or stopping to doctor the leak. Given the visual of a crowd of hikers stumbling upon the repair process, I chose to press on regardless. The damage was done. I would have to bear it.

Hour 4

There is one final uphill section of about 1.5 miles. I take it one step at a time, stopping every five to six steps to get my heart rate back down below 200. My knees were killing me. My back was killing me. My feet felt kind of funny. I looked and noticed blood oozing from sneakers. This was the mountain's final chance at beating me. I laced my shoes up tighter and pressed on. The squelching sound from the blood in my shoes echoed to my whistling of the theme from "Bridge Over the River Kwai."

Hour 5

I could see off in the distance a road with traffic. This did not lighten my mood any. I began to threaten passing hikers who looked like they were enjoying themselves. The dark thoughts of harming the trip organizers were now coming back. I reasoned that if I could do anything on the remaining downhill section of this trip, it was to impress on the hapless hikers the horrors with which they were about to be faced. I was as John the Baptist, a voice crying in the wilderness. None would listen to me; they all pressed on up the mountain, smiling, unknowing and unaware of their fate.

Hour 6

I had never kissed a car before this day. People stared oddly at me as I knelt before the 300M and wept. I finally turned and sat looking back up the death trail. I nodded knowingly as the small children and grandparents set out on the same hike that had almost taken my life. They, too, were on their way to the Chalet of death. If they only knew what was in store for them.

So what have I learned from this experience?

1. The words "Walk," "Mountain," and "Chalet" should never be used in the same sentence and have been stricken from my personal vocabulary.

2. Anyone who will pay $85 per person to experience what I went through, "just ain't right."

3. Near death experiences tend to change your perspective on personal violence.

4. I need to do more weight lifting than just "getting out of bed" each morning.

5. The description "Romantic Night" is a misrepresentation when you and your spouse share a room with "Ted and Alice" in the bunk up above.

6. The next time my wife tells me we're going to a remote chalet for the night, there had better be a donkey, lama, motorcycle, car or helicopter involved in the transportation process.

Life Lesson Number 497

—

"Bob the Campsite Remora"

Day 1

We had planned a quiet weekend of camping for the Memorial Day weekend. Just our family and a group of friends were to come along for a relaxing get away. Being out of work, I went up early Friday and set up camp. This worked out well and allowed us to avoid setting up camp in the dark like so many other weekend camping warriors.

After completing our setup, I sat in my chair in our magnificently laid out campsite. As I did so, I looked across the way at a small tent hastily pitched standing alone. It had obviously been put up early to hold a site for someone. I could tell by the quality of the tent that it was brand new and that the person erecting the tent had not followed instructions. Interesting, I thought, I wonder who will camp there? I dismissed the tent and the profile that I began to put together of its owner.

About 8:00 pm Friday night a small truck rolls up to the small tent site across from us and a man and his eight-year-old son bail out. We shall call them Bob and Son of Bob from this point on. They start throwing out what appeared to be cardboard boxes of new equipment: tents, lanterns, beds, sleeping bags, etc. Initially their antics were quite amusing but after a while I stop paying attention to the Keystone Cop activity across the way and got back to reading my book by the fire.

As I begin to read, I hear, "May I enter the campsite?" from the gentleman across the way. Such an odd statement, nothing like "Hello" or "Hi." Something was amiss here. My "warning sign clock" clicked off zero and set itself to one.

I turn to see a burly balding man and his son standing at the edge of our campsite. He looked harmless enough, so I said, "Come on in neighbor and what can I do for you?" In hindsight I would regret having said these words all week-end. This was my first introduction to "Bob—the campsite Remora!"

Now, you may not know what a remora is. It is a species that attaches itself to a host and sucks its very existence from that host. It does not feed itself, it does not clean itself, it does not support itself, it just exists on the host body. The host, unable to detach the remora, must live with the discomfort forever! As the largest being around, I was naturally chosen for whatever tasty morsels might fall from our ample supply of campsite goodies. I was targeted, I was acquired, and the suc-tion cups had been attached.

But I digress. Bob seemed none to bright as he and Son of Bob made them-selves at home around our fire. Bob was holding a box that contained a Coleman lantern. He said that he had no idea of how to put it together and that he needed my help. (Warning sign clock checks to two but is ignored.) In my mind I am running through the age-old sayings such as "everyman must carry his own water" and "you can give a man a fish and he will eat for a day, but if you teach a man to fish…" You know how it goes. Mistakenly, I reached out and took the carton from him. I determined to put the lantern together for him as a gesture of good will. In truth, I was feeding him fish for a day.

I whipped the parts out, assembled them hastily (amid the oohs and aahs of the owner as to my prowess). Having made the hasty assembly, I lit the lantern up for him and then listened for an hour to how "he didn't know how to do stuff like that." During this time Son of Bob is playing in the fire, entering our tents and generally making himself at home by requesting food and drink from some very disgruntled ladies. Several times I thought Bob was about to leave as we had given him the universal "Well, we need to do this…(insert any activity here)…now!" hint that any normal person can pick up on.

Finally he reaches down and lays his hand on top of the lantern. Flat, palm down. (The "Warning sign clock" clicks up another notch.) You could hear the flesh sizzle as the Coleman brand was permanently embedded in his palm. He dances around begging for ice and assistance to soothe his injury. We hesitantly give first aid fearing that like a lion receiving aid to remove a thorn, we too would hold a "Special Place" in this person's weekend. (Warning sign clock checks up yet another notch). I note to myself that we are now officially in trouble with this guy.

After about an hour of on-again off-again "exits," Bob and son of Bob head back to their campsite. After breathing a sigh of relief, I do the "elevator don't go all the way to the top" signal to the rest of our group and they agree.

As the evening progressed we were visited many times by Bob and Son of Bob. Mostly they just made conversation, but occasionally they sought advice. In the rare moments when he was actually at his campsite, we were amused by Bob's attempts to put together camping chairs and start a fire. As the evening progressed and no measurable warmth could be gained from the still unlit fire, we looked and watched as Bob and Son of Bob stood looking longingly at us, sitting around our lovely warm fire and munching on our wonderful snacks.

When Bob made a final attempt to visit our fire, our group hastily made for the tents and feigned sleep.

Day 2

We wake early (around 8:00 am) to find Son of Bob in our campsite waiting for us to get up. He asks us for breakfast. He tells us that they have no food. We say, "No, sorry, we only have enough for our group! You need to eat with your family." We find ourselves under siege. They have us encircled. Our supply lines have been cut off. All exits are covered. We settle in for the duration.

Bob approaches, "May I enter the campsite?" At this question, our camp partner's dachshund wiener dog goes wild, causing Bob to stand back from our site. "We have found our means of defense," I tell the others and myself. We may make it through today. Any self-respecting camper with a Leatherman Tool, some duct tape, and a wiener dog could hold this guy off for hours. Bob stands and waits patiently for an answer to his odd question. Finally, giving in to the awkwardness of the situation, I ask, "What can I do for you NOW?"

At this point we learn that Bob and Son of Bob are novice campers. They had no equipment so everything (and I mean everything) they had in the truck was new. About five hundred dollars worth of camping equipment by his own admission. He asks if I had something to drive in tent pegs, as the ground was "hard." I began to ask myself why he needed a mallet to drive pegs when his tent was already up. Bob answered before I could voice the question by saying that he had bought a bigger tent. Just what a father and son needs—a three-room tent that will sleep twelve. I offer him my persuader "mallet" (handed down from my grandfather to me) to pound pegs. Later on I would consider pounding him with the same mallet. It was returned chipped to pieces by the steel stakes that he had driven deeply into the hardened soil.

Bob was poetry in motion. Since I had feigned sleep in my chair and the others at our site had sought shelter inside the tents, Bob had no one to help him put up the "Large Tent." He was a master at his trade. Everyone that went by his campsite was stopped for help. "Can you help me put this together? Can you show me how to do this? Does this go here?" He organized a guy from a couple of sites up to put up his huge new three-room tent for him. Bob did not lift a finger. He just stood there asking questions about spiders and anti-venoms, snakes, and car tires. Finally, after much sweating on the part of the helper, (and no sweat from Bob), the large tent was up and ready. Bob and Son of Bob moved into the new digs leaving the smaller tent to hold the excess equipment purchased for the trip.

Bob's reputation was starting to spread. I think the other campers had figured out what he was like and were making adjustments. You could see them hesitate as they walked by on the road, waiting for that moment when Bob was occupied or looking longingly at us. When he was distracted, they would rush by. Many changed directions and went out of their way to avoid contact.

We had no protection. We were in plain and direct sight. Every spare moment Bob had that Saturday was spent at our site. By now, it was all elbows and knees trying to get into the tents when he made his way over. It didn't matter. You had to go to the bathroom some time. In rare moments when we broke into the sunshine he caught us. You would feign a route, change direction like a running back, but he always caught you.

Finally, he took his son out for lunch (since he had no food). This was our chance to get on with life. During this break we had additional friends show up from Indiana. The father and five-year-old son had not camped out before so we invited them to stay the night with us. They agreed.

When Bob and Son of Bob returned early in the evening, Son of Bob was drawn to our new young guest as a moth to flame. As children will, our new five-year-old mentioned "Smores" to Son of Bob. This delicacy drove the child wild. Every few minutes he would ask if we were going to make "smores." Our answer, "Not until after you have had your dinner!" So we dutifully sent Son of Bob back to his camp to get dinner. Having watched the previous evening's experience we knew that this would be a monumental task that would take all night.

In the meantime, Bob had been shopping for food. Not just regular camping food like wieners, hamburgers or bacon and eggs, he had purchased a large quantity of fish fillets. Now up until this point, Bob had not had any cooking utensils or stoves in sight, so we wondered how he was going to cook the fish.

"May I enter the camp?" said Bob. With gritted teeth I replied, "How can we help you?" Bob responded that he had purchased a deep fryer (that's right, the expensive gas bottle driven model) just to cook the fish in oil. (Warning sign clock checks up another notch.) His naivety knows no bounds. He tells me that he needs me to help put it together. "Of course!" I said, determined that I would do anything to help him stay occupied in his own campsite. So I set off to help put the deep fryer together. This task took three minutes as all the pieces were made to sit on top of each other. I struck "Rocket Scientist" from Bob's possible occupation list.

Bob commenced cooking fish and kept yelling to everyone that hesitantly passed by that he had fish if they wanted some. He approached us again. "May I enter the camp?" said Bob. We did not reply. "I have some fish if you would like it." We politely declined and tried not to make eye contact with him. Our visiting five-year-old yells that he would love some fish, so off he goes and indulges at Bob's camp.

We try to keep still and quiet so that we can now have an evening together, Bobless. It would not be so. Bob was back with Son of Bob. I grab the smores makings and race through the construction of the sticky snack just to get them out of our hair. We really wanted to play cards quietly, without interruption from Bob. This was not to be. Bob pulls up a chair and takes over the conversation with our guest. By the end of the evening, we have gone to bed to get away from Bob, and he has invited our guest to sleep in his extra tent. Our guest has to go as Bob would not take no for an answer. I considered our guests a sacrificial offering. It was every man for himself now. They could take care of themselves.

Day 3

Breakfast is cereal today. I know, because as I wake up I hear Son of Bob complaining about us only having cereal for breakfast. I slap my head and cover my eyes. I have to leave the tent sometime today! Or do I? I get up and do my best W.C. Fields impersonation and tell the kid to "Get out of here and go eat with your Dad!" Son of Bob tells us that all they have are potato chips. Tough!

As we finish breakfast, Bob pays us another visit so that he can lay out in detail his plans for today. I can tell that he is trying to get us to divulge our agenda so that he can sync up his plans with ours. Thankfully, none of us broke under the endless repetitive questions. Security was intact. I had had all the questioning that I could take. I try, and succeed, to excuse myself, get my shower goodies, and slide away to the bathroom (thinking that I might get a few minutes alone). I make a break for it and load up my fresh clothes in the shower stall and settle in for a few quiet moments in the throne room. At last I am alone. "May I enter the Bathroom?" came the call from the door. Is it possible to experience both despair and panic at the same time? I freeze like a rabbit in a spotlight. I sat quietly hoping that he would just go away. I was wrong. He wants to talk as I sit and contemplate.

Now, there are some things in my life that are mutually exclusive. You know, one thing at a time. Talking was not something that I wanted to do at this moment of meditation. I tried monosyllabic answers. This failed. I determined that I needed to change location. "Keep the target moving," I told myself. I hastily completed my work and moved to the showers.

Like SAM missiles locked on to a Tomcat at mach 1.3, Bob and Son of Bob take up residence in the stall next to me. They were locked on and my countermeasures were failing. I disrobe and quickly move my soap and shampoo to the shower stall, placing them on top of the ledge. I did this because there were no shelves in the shower. This was a mistake.

"Can I borrow your hair shampoo?" Bob calls out from the next shower. "We forgot to bring our shower stuff with us." This came as no surprise to me. Before I can say no, the hair shampoo disappears into the next stall. I quickly hide my soap (there are some things I will not share). This has gone far enough. I finish showering (after begging for my shampoo), hastily dry, dress and run back to camp, leaving them to use paper towels to dry themselves. No way were they going to get my towel, comb and deodorant.

In the few moments of Boblessness that we had, a defensive plan was set in place. It was about to start storming, so we determined that we must secure the perimeter not to mention keep out the rain. At this point we circled the wagons (drove the large van in front of the tent) draped two huge tarpaulins over the whole campsite, and tied them down. We set the wiener dog at the one entry point to the north (facing away from Bob's camp). We had sealed off all visual contact with his site and made all entry points except one impassable. If the wiener dog did its work we determined that this might just work!

What followed were a few hours of campsite bliss. Bob took the perimeter setup as a hint and headed off in to town to purchase some more expensive equipment for people to assemble. From our perspective it was his plan to lure unsuspecting males into his camp using the new equipment, get them to help put it together, and then bore them to death.

By late evening we were relaxing. We knew there was activity on the outskirts of our perimeter but we did not care. "May I enter the camp?" came the call from the north entrance. I knew who it was as the wiener dog was about to burst a vessel trying to tear into our intruder. In retrospect the men believe that the women were the ones that finally broke down, subdued the wiener dog, and let him back in. It didn't matter. Our lives were over. My "Warning sign clock" could be used as a fan. It was spinning wildly.

Like the British troops before the Continental Armies, the fall back began as he made his way through the campsite. We surrendered it all as one by one we yawned, stretched and feigned either sleep or death. The tents quickly filled leaving Bob the conqueror. He had won. There were no more defenses. We had tried everything. We were under occupation. Nothing worked. So we slept.

Day 4

As dawn broke, I uncovered my eyes and listened for Son of Bob or Bob in the campsite. No movement was heard. During the night I had struck upon the strategy of "Run Silent Run Deep." We were going to rig for silent running so as to avoid being detected by our tormentor.

Using this latest strategy, we made it all the way through breakfast before a slight clank of a skillet against a metal stove gave us away. "May I enter the camp?" A quick glance at our campmates sealed the day's fate. In what was later looked upon as a logistics miracle, we broke camp (around Bob) and retreated to the sanctity of our vehicles. The organizers of the Normandy evacuations would have been proud.

As we drove off, he stood there. I don't know if the look on his face was a look of victory or a look of fear at finding himself alone and reliant upon his own wits for the rest of the day. As we drove off, I felt some small victory had been had as we had made a clean getaway. Then guilt began to set in. Bob had turned, and was heading for the next site up. I will never forget the look of fear on the faces of that poor family.

So what have I learned from this experience?

1. People are stupid. At least some of them are. Well, maybe just one.

2. Proper prior planning prevents…ah, who am I kidding; nothing could have kept this guy out!

3. The apple doesn't fall far from the tree.

4. There is no relationship between "the quality of the camping experience" and "the amount of money spent to set that experience up."

5. State Parks should require deep background and personality checks on all future campsite registrations.

6. I must research if State Parks really mean "No firearms" and whether they had Bob and Son of Bob in mind when they made that decision.

7. Further, was this rule set up to protect the campers, or Bob and Son of Bob?

8. I will be adding cyanide pills to our camping equipment medical kit (to prevent death by boredom).

Life Lesson Number 499

—

"Two Timing Man!"

I have to admit "there are now two women in my life" and I love them both more than life itself. I have lived with one for twenty-three years, but it is the other that has gone through some changes lately. My problem is that I can't decide what to do with this new love. She has crept into my heart over the last thirteen years. It was all quite unexpected. I never thought that I would be faced with this dilemma. I was about to lose her to another man and couldn't face the thought of letting her go. Now before you get all hoity-toity about me two timing my wife I want you to know that we're talking about my daughter here. To be precise, it is my "about-to-be-thirteen-year-old" daughter.

When the birthday invitations went out for her party, I didn't expect to see boys on the list. Boys were icky and had germs the last time I noticed my daughter's reaction to them. At the last birthday party sleep-over for all her friends, the boys were only mentioned in hushed tones. I guess things change when you turn thirteen. When I asked her about the boys being at the party she just rolled her eyes and said, "Oh, Daddy!" I guess she thought I understood the importance of this transition. So I set out to find what was planned for the birthday bash.

After a little research I found out that the party was this next weekend; it was a skating party and that not only would there be boys at the party, but that "the boy" would be at the party. "And so it begins!" I moaned to myself. He was the love of her life (this week) and they could not wait to go skating together. Wait a minute? Skating? I suspect that a little more preteen forethought than usual had gone into the planning of this party. Skating is fun, but more so if there are boys to push around and joke with and heaven forbid that I gag as I say it, "hold hands with." I was mortified because now I had competition for my daughter. I would not go down without a fight.

In the few days that I had before the party, I took it upon myself to plan a suitable response to any move that the pre-pubescent little punk might put on my darling daughter. "Sitting," was okay, I reasoned, as long as there was "no touching." "Looking" was okay as long as it was at her face. "Touching" was definitely out of the question. Kissing was, well, too horrifying to even comprehend just yet. So I concerned myself with planning for the inevitable "hand holding" that was to occur.

I struck upon several plans, which mostly centered on causing scenes of pure embarrassment for my daughter, thus alienating her friends. No, that would ruin her social life and therefore make me miserable. I then moved on to covert actions of intervention. The first of these covert actions was the old "accidentally" throwing myself down in front of them, causing a massive pile up, probable injury to the young whiskerless lad, and a quick trip to the emergency room for him. But that might hurt my daughter. What to do? What to do?

Then I thought of the old psychological move where you slash your finger across the throat area when only the boy could see you. I worried and thought that perhaps that was too suggestive! Besides, there were too many witnesses for me to start cleaning my Crocodile Dundee knife at the skate center anyway.

I finally settled on the "I'm-watching-you hand signal" where you point two fingers at your eyes, mouth the words, "I'm watching you!" and then point at the culprit with a look of pure evil in your eyes. This move was pretty effective if you ask me, because I even scared myself as I practiced it in the mirror in our bathroom.

So we were off to the skate center for the party to begin.

I just want to say that as a father with a new teenage daughter, I was somewhat surprised at just how much had changed between the ages of twelve and thirteen years. These kids had changed from giggling babies the year before into hormonally crazed women.

As the music cranked up and the loud beat kicked in, I marveled at the maneuvering on the skate center floor as the boys and girls circled each other in what appeared to be some primitive primordial tribal dance. It was definitely a tribal dance, because the boys had dressed up for it. They had put on their best tribal baggy pants and underpants for all to see and had spent considerable time in positioning those hats in odd and precarious positions. They were not unlike a bunch of male emus preening their feathers prior to a night out with the girls.

The primordial dance started out with the boys on one side whispering about the girls and the girls on the other side whispering about the boys. They were circling, circling, and circling, each group keeping to opposite sides of the floor and then without warning "Attila the hormone kicked in." The boys swooped around the girls at high speed showing off their manly abilities and prowess on roller skates. In the young men's eyes skate speed and wild arm movements were obviously associated with their ability to impress the women and therefore propagate the next generation of the species. To me they looked like over sexed bees ready to extract pollen from some unsuspecting flower, and that flower was my daughter.

A change of pace was in order. The loud pounding music was stopped and all gathered around the cake to sing happy birthday, eat, drink and open presents. This I could control. It did not go unnoticed that the predator man-child strategically placed himself next to the birthday girl for all the pictures and ceremonies to follow. He was good, I had to give him that. We both eyed each other and nodded our agreement to take this to the next level. Gunslinger music wafted through my head as we both mentally circled the object of our affection. I was there to protect Miss Kitty; he was here to take her away.

When the presents were being opened, the man-child sat patiently waiting for us to pass Tabitha each of the presents. I knew which one was his and I hid it. Childish? Yes, but very effective. The look on his face as I said that we were out of presents gave me some satisfaction. The ruse would not hold, however, as Dee Ann had noticed what was going on and made me hand it over. Reluctantly I did so. (She did have to hit me in the arm several times before I gave in though.)

All her friends were giggling and smiling as she opened the present. I waited and was stunned by what he gave Tabitha. This guy was a professional, I had to give him that. In the card game of gifts for thirteen-year-old girls, he went straight for the wild card: "The silver locket on a neck chain." Now I ask you, "What chance does a father have against that?" I could have written a check for a million dollars right there and it would have wafted to the floor forgotten as she swooned over the thirteen dollar Wal-Mart necklace that he gave her. I rolled my eyes and got the laser look from Dee Ann. What else could go wrong tonight? I was apparently losing control.

Then it happened. The lights dimmed. The slow romantic music started. I knew what was coming, but it was too late. It was the couples skate and the man-child escorted my baby girl out onto the skate floor. With a look back over their shoulders at me, they both set off skating side by side. No touching, just skating. Wait, I was wrong. He reached out and took her hand. With that motion she looked lovingly into his eyes and they skated on.

Tears welled up in my eyes. That was all there was to this little competition. He had won. I sat there watching them skate around and watching my life flash before me. With each circle of the skating rink different memories came to me:

- I saw a three-year-old blond-headed girl in pink Barbie skates holding her Daddy's hand as she learned to skate for the first time.

- I saw a five-year-old blond-headed girl at a friend's birthday skate party waving to her Daddy each time she confidently went around the skate rink.

- I saw an eight-year-old blond-headed girl enter the speed skate race at the skating rink and come in second. When the race was over she was so excited, and I was the first person she rushed over to tell.

- I saw a ten-year-old blond-headed girl ice-skating with her girl friends giggling at how silly her Daddy was when he worried about her falling over but still needing a cuddle to make it feel better.

- Today I saw a thirteen-year-old blond-headed girl skating around the rink holding hands with her first love.

For the first time in my life, I realized that someday soon I wouldn't be the center of her life anymore. There will be someone more important to her than me. I decided right there and then that I needed to let go and let her grow up. I needed to let her make choices in her life, and hopefully with some guidance early on, those choices will involve her meeting and loving good people.

I nodded acceptance to the man-child. He smiled and nodded at me as I gave him the "I'm watching you!" hand signal. The uneasy truce had set in. I could now make plans on how I would introduce him to my gun collection, my prowess with heavy digging equipment, and the twenty-two ways that I could kill a man with a sharp number two lead pencil. Things might be looking up.

So what have I learned from this experience?

1. The tribal dance will never be dead.

2. Daddies hear gunslinger music in their heads when they look at boys wooing their daughters.

3. Dress codes change from generation to generation.

4. Rule number 1—No Touching!

5. Rule number 2—If he makes her cry, I make him cry!

6. If you must show me your underwear, just wear them on the outside of your pants.

7. Hats are not a fashion accessory, they are just hats. Traditionally, they do not serve any mating ritual function.

8. Men are pigs. I know, I used to be a man before I got married.

9. Daddies, in the thirteen-year-old gift game of cards, be the first to throw the wild card.

10. No matter how old she gets, she will always be my baby girl.

Life Lesson Number 500

—

"Sex, Lies and Videotape"

I stood in line at our high schools general assembly, our seventh grade class way at the back of the quadrangle where all the plebiscite classes were found. The Principal was up at the lectern rattling on and on and on about something that didn't really matter to me when BOOM! I noticed that Debbie Bolin had legs. Now, let me tell you this, guys, she didn't just have regular legs, she had really lovely curvaceous legs. "Why the leg fascination all of a sudden?" I thought to myself. "She has always had those legs; what is different about them now?" Little did I know at the time, but "Attila the hormone" had just kicked into high gear and I was now in for the chemically imbalanced roller coaster ride called puberty.

I shouldn't have been surprised about this change. I had been told that puberty was coming and that it should not be feared. I guess what bothered me about the whole puberty thing was the veil of secrecy under which it was held. The whole sex thing appeared to be a conspiracy on the part of the parents to keep us in the dark. It was the tribal way.

Sex education in the Shepherd household was for the most part a relatively hands off situation. Mum and Dad had never spoken of sex openly. I didn't even dare to acknowledge that I had a passing interest in some of the young ladies in my class that were really nice to me. That would tell Mum and Dad that I was indeed a sexual being, and that was a bad thing. In sixth grade, prior to my first real boys and girls birthday party at my friends house, my mother sat me down and said, "Ian, your father and I have decided that you need to know about sex."

I can remember cringing at the word. I had always cringed whenever anyone said that word because I had been caught in fourth grade looking up the word "sex" in my dictionary. I was so ashamed at having been caught that I didn't notice the smirk on the teacher's face as he pointed out to everyone that I had been caught looking up "that sex word." That traumatic event had stayed with me for the next two years. I had never really recovered from the embarrassment of it all. Whenever I did something stupid in class, the kids always referred to me as "that kid that looked up the word sex in the dictionary." It appeared that I was doomed to carry that label forever.

So this was it. The big sex talk that I knew was coming was finally here. I steeled myself for what I thought was going to be a long and tedious discussion of different types of body equipment, fluid exchanges, hair growing, and all sorts of horrid things about girls, when my mother blurted out, "So we are sending you to a special movie at school."

That was it, a movie? How bad could that be? Mum said that I would get to go on my own and find out all about how babies were made. To a sixth grader "the alone" thing was a big win. At least I wouldn't have to sit next to my father when they started talking about the birds and the bees.

So off I went to the movie. It was really quite a let-down for someone who had finally had his interest peaked in finding out more about sex. In typical late 60's and early 70's non-offensive fashion, the movie talked about a few distant biological functions, vaguely described some anatomy changes, and then ended up with a discussion of the birds and the bees. It left me more dazed and confused about the whole situation than when I had walked into the stupid movie. All I found out was that I apparently had "on board" some "important equipment" that might be useful "someday," but I didn't have the instruction manual to figure out how it all worked. Well, at least the instruction manual had some pages missing.

When I got home from the movie, my mother sat me down at the kitchen table. She was sitting there peeling potatoes, carrots and pumpkin for our dinner. Having situated her embarrassed blonde-haired boy across from her, she started to ask me questions about the movie. "So, what did you learn?" she asked openly. I stammered around and said, "Not much!"

Well, apparently this little revelation from the blonde-headed boy caused Mum to rethink the whole "let someone else do the sex education thing." She looked at me as she quietly worked at peeling the vegetables. She said, "Son, there are only five things that you need to know when it comes to sex!" She then proceeded to list the five secret keys to a good healthy sex life. These had obviously been imparted to her through some secret ceremony with her own parents and had been handed down through the ages. I was about to learn something. I leaned in to listen closely. Each revelation was accompanied by a knowing wink or nod. She began:

1. If you touch yourself, you will go blind.
2. If you ever sleep with a girl, you could end up with the pox.

3. If you don't get the pox, you could get the dibs and dabs.

4. If you don't get the dibs and dabs, you could get something much worse.

And the piece of resistance:

5. If you ever get a girl pregnant, I will…!

Number five's silent ending was visually reinforced by my mother chopping through a carrot on the cutting board with her sharp little vegetable knife and burning her laser eyes into my forehead. I can remember my eyes bulging as I gulped air at this revelation and carefully crossed my legs. This was serious stuff. So that is what sex education is all about: "Fear!"

To any normal eleven-year-old boy the above discussion may have just been filed away as a humorous anecdote of a parent's attempt to reinforce the serious nature of sex and its responsibilities. I was not normal. I had an active imagination: so many questions and yet so few answers.

Questions like:

1. If I could not touch myself, how could I go to the bathroom without going blind?

2. When did this blindness start?

3. Was it already too late for me? After all, I had been going to the bathroom on and off since birth. I held up my hand in front of my eyes to get a finger count. I could still see, but I really did need to go to the toilet. I might need a white cane by bedtime tonight.

4. What new procedures would I have to deduce regarding bathroom etiquette to resolve this "touching" situation when going to the toilet?

5. If I sleep with a girl I will get the pox?

6. If you're sleeping, how bad could that be?

7. I had no control over sleeping. I had to sleep, didn't I?

8. When you say sleep with a girl, is that in the same bed, room, house, or street? I might already be doomed. There were several girls living on my street.

9. What is "the pox?" The mere sound of the word drove chills up my spine. Visions of plague and pestilence filled my poor little mind.

10. How do you get the pox just from sleeping with a girl? Obviously some horrendous chemical reaction to an accidental female touch?

11. If a girl sneaks up and touches you while you're asleep, do you still get the pox? I had no lock on my bedroom door. I determined that I might never sleep again for fear of being ambushed by a girl.

12. If the pox is a bad thing, then obviously the next level of torment is the dibs and dabs, right?

13. What exactly are the dibs and dabs?

14. Are dibs worse than dabs and when combined do they compound each other?

15. Where do you get them and if you have them what do they do to you?

16. How do you tell the difference between a dib and a dab?

17. And what could be "Worse" than the dibs and dabs? Death?

18. I have to break the code?

19. This is a code?

20. Isn't it?

The only thing that I was pretty sure of was that there was no way I was ever going to get a girl pregnant. That little vision and its consequences were forever burned into my poor little psyche. It's pretty amazing how clear "vague innuendo" can be when accompanied by a visual reinforcement.

So there it was: the secret of the ages revealed in mysterious codes of rhyming slang, folkloric diseases, and visual innuendo. I determined right there and then that I would not put any child of mine through this painful deductive course of self-exploration and vague explanation. I was going to be more up front about the whole process if I could ever figure it out for myself.

And so, when my own son, Ethan, was ten-years-old, I read in the paper that the local hospital was having a class for fathers and sons dealing with sex education, I rushed to sign us up for the class. This was going to be great. It was a three-week course for the sons and a four-week course for the fathers. As fathers we got to go a week early to see what our sons were going to cover in the additional three weeks. I was pretty pleased with myself. This was way better than any movie and dinner table discussion of dibs and dabs, pox and pregnancy. I wanted only the best for my ten-year-old son and he was getting a medical professional to show us the ropes.

Ethan had not displayed any interest at all in girls but had started to ask a few questions about where babies really came from. These questions had started when his older sister and mother had spent four weeks in mother and daughter classes covering the same topics. When I approached him about the class, he seemed a little embarrassed about the whole thing but said that he was willing to go "If I went with him!"

On the first night of class we entered the lecture auditorium to find that about ten other father and son groups were there. As luck would have it, one of Ethan's best friends and his father were there as well. Seeing a friendly face and relaxing a little, Ethan settled into the large executive chair next to me and leaned back waiting for the doctor to come in and start.

When the doctor entered the room, it went deathly quiet. Only the fathers were smiling and relaxed and you could see the fear and apprehension on the face of every son there. Ethan sat deathly still, his little ashen face a statue of fear and apprehension. The doctor began, "I would like to welcome each of you here today. We are going to talk about sex."

At the first mention of the word sex, Ethan's mouth cracked a little at the side and a little nervous giggle emerged from his mouth. "He he he he heh!" The doctor ignored it and moved on. "We will be talking about the anatomy of the male," at which point the doctor drew down a lifelike nude chart of the male human anatomy. The quiet child beside me allowed another much longer giggle accompanied by the occasional snort to emerge from his tightly clenched mouth, all the while trying to suppress a smile that was beginning to emerge on his face.

The doctor went on, "When looking at the male we will talk about the most important sex organ. The male testes!" At that time the doctor slapped the testicular area of the chart with a long pointer. This was too much for Ethan. Grasping the arms of the executive chair he began to laugh and snort uncontrollably. Nothing that he did could stop him from his nervous giggle. The doctor broke in. "Yes, yes, yes, it's okay to laugh at the word testes." At the mere mention of the word again, Ethan fell forward, face down on the desk, howling laughter, and completely out of control. The doctor finally added, "Yes it's okay to laugh, although it appears that Ethan is doing enough of that for all of us!" "That's my boy," I thought to myself as I flashed back to my movie and dinner table discussion with Mum. "He will settle down," I told myself, and he did.

As the weeks went on, nothing escaped Ethan's attention in the class. He picked up all the terminology. He could discuss in great detail the cycles of women and the impregnation process with a detail that approached medical genius as far as I was concerned. He could openly discuss the physiological changes that his body had gone through and would be going through. He had absolutely no qualms at all about talking about anything to do with sex. He was an open book. He said what he thought; he questioned what he did not know; he accepted the answers that I gave to difficult questions. I was the proud father of a son who could discuss any sexual topic openly at the age of ten.

Now, when I say that he discussed things "openly" with our family, I mean "openly." Things have been so "open" lately that I have begun to feel a little out of sorts about some of the discussions that my son feels comfortable talking to me about. Discussions like: how many fathers do you know that have their sons walk by them in the morning, high-five them and say, "Had a wet dream last night, Dad!" As a father, what do you say to that? "Good for you son?" Or when you're traveling on your way to Great Grandma's house and your son interrupts from the back of the car asking what he should do about his "little problem." "What little problem?" I innocently asked. "Dad, I have an erection and it appears to have a mind of its own," he said to the whole family in the car. So many little pearls of wisdom from the mouths of babes!

From a father's perspective and based on my conservative nature, I think that I have reached the point where I am willing to discuss sex education with anyone. I have covered all the hard stuff with my son. But do you know what? The next time I am asked about sex and the discussion of it makes me feel uncomfortable, I will respond, "No worries, I can talk about sex. You know what, there are only five things that you need to know when it comes to sex:

1. If you touch yourself, you will go blind.
2. If you ever sleep with a girl, you could end up with the pox.
3. If you don't get the pox, you could get the dibs and dabs.
4. If you don't get the dibs and dabs, you could get something much worse...

And the piece of resistance:

5. If you ever get a girl pregnant, I will...CHOP!

By the time they figure all five out, they will be married, have kids of their own, and be facing the same questions themselves.

So what have I learned from this experience?

1. Fear puberty.

2. Sex education is an adult conspiracy to confuse the young.

3. We need to get sex off the front page of our minds and back into the deep recesses of mystery and folklore where it really belongs.

4. When you buy your next dictionary, black out the word "sex" and its definition with a felt tip marker. You could save an eight-year-old from a fate worse than death.

5. When you mother asks you if you learned anything in sex education just say "YES!"

6. Veiled innuendo and mysteries are often better than the truth.

7. Going to the toilet will not send you blind. However, there seems to be a correlation between getting older, spending longer in the toilet, developing hemorrhoids, and your eyesight gradually going bad.

8. The people next to you frown upon a "hands-off" contortionist act at the urinal.

9. You cannot get "the pox" from sleeping. What a relief that was after many sleepless nights!

10. The answer is "a Bed," not the room, house or street.

11. "The Pox"—apparently a colorful description of any generic social disease.

12. "Dibs and Dabs"—rhyming slang for "the crabs" or body lice.

13. You cannot tell the difference between a dib and a dab. Well, at least not without a very good microscope and the Eighth Edition of "Simon's Field Guide to Sexing Body Lice."

14. The secret tribal code of "Sex Education" can never really be fully broken. Let's keep it that way.

15. I could never eat carrots after that day without thinking of certain consequences.

16. When the tough questions get asked, fall back on folklore, innuendo and fear. It worked for me.

Life Lesson Number 501

—

"Whisker Kisses"

He sat down in the old chair at the door to the farmhouse and beckoned me to come over and get on his knee. I hurried over to him and climbed up on his knee waiting for what was about to happen. Leaning down and reaching out his rough old hand, he put one finger under my chin, lifting it up to see where my beard was. He would look closely for a minute and then exclaim, "There's nothing there yet!" I would scrunch my chin down knowing what was about to happen. With that, Fardie Shep would take his whiskery chin and rub it on my chin and cheeks as I giggled my delight at the attention. "I guess I better plant some whiskers for you!" he would say. "When you grow up you need to plant whiskers on your children, just like I did with your Dad."

This had become a ritual with us when we went up to see Fardie and Nana Shep at the farm in Kurrajong. As we left that day in 1962, he rubbed my head and told me to be good. That was my last whisker kiss. It was the last time I saw my grandfather alive. He died later that week.

The Australian male is a funny thing. So bound by manly stereotypes and yet determined to break them in many ways. I can't ever remember my grandfather giving me a kiss or telling me that he loved me. That would be too out of character for a tough old farmer from the sixties, and yet here in his own special way he was telling me that I was special and that he loved me. He showed me by his actions.

As I grew up my Dad reminded me a lot of my grandfather. He was different in some ways and yet still he was the man's man, bound by what was deemed acceptable Aussie male behavior at the time. On many occasions Dad would wrestle us kids on the floor, and when he finally had tickled us into submission he would lean over and plant the whiskers on us. It didn't matter if you were a boy or girl you got "the whiskers." He would plant them there on Susan (our sister), just so her kids would one day get them. My brother and I were mercilessly whiskered, so that our beards would "come in" one day. Dad would then tell us to pass them on to our kids when we had them.

As we grew up and left home, the ritual passed on to me. When my children were born and old enough to wrestle I would do the same thing that my father had done. When the kids could finally take no more tickles I would put my chin on their chins and give them a whisker kiss. They would laugh and giggle at the thought of having whiskers planted. I would tell them that they had to pass them on to their kids so that the whisker line would continue through the generations. My grandfather gave them to my Dad and my Dad had given them to me. Now I was giving my whiskers to them. Both promised me that they would do so when they grew up.

Things changed when I moved to America. Dad realized that he couldn't whisker kiss his old son and grandkids over a distance of 12,000 miles. He became comfortable with telling us in words what he thought about us. We would talk every few days on the phone as he kept up with our lives and kept in touch. We never said goodbye without an "I love you" and an instruction to hug the kids and tell them that he loved them, too. He missed us and wanted us to know it. Times had changed, and so had my father.

He sat in his chair that February eighth morning waiting for me to say good-bye. It was the end of a quick visit back home to Australia. I went over to Dad and hugged him. I told him that I loved him and I kissed him on the cheek. As I did so tears welled in his eyes. He said, "I love you, too." I went over to Mum and kissed and hugged her goodbye and told her that I loved her. She responded that she loved me, too.

As I walked towards the door, I turned and saw him stand up and look at me as if he had something else to say. I walked back and kissed his cheek and hugged him again. As I hugged him, he rubbed his beard against the side of my face the way he used to when I was a little boy and said, "Tell the kids I love them." I knew what he was doing. In his own way he was saying goodbye. It was my last whisker kiss and the one that I will always remember.

<u>*So what have I learned from this experience?*</u>

1. Someone doesn't have to say; "I love you" for you to know you're loved.

2. Change is okay.

3. You don't have to live up to everyone else's standard. Make your own and be comfortable with it.

4. Everyone should start a simple family tradition.

5. Whisker kisses are fun. Go ahead, enjoy!

6. Remember, you never know when you might be getting your last whisker kiss.

Life Lesson Number 504

—

"When you need it most!"

We arrived home from church at about 7:40 pm that Sunday night. It was June 30, 2002. We were tired. We had been traveling all day back from Montgomery, Alabama, and had decided to go directly to church rather than go home and have to go back out. As we came in our door, I could see the message machine light blinking. As I walked past it, I punched the button to half-heartedly listen to those annoying messages as I dumped the dregs of travel on the floor

I could tell immediately that something was wrong. My sister, Susan, had left an urgent message. She said that they had been trying to get in touch with me on my cell phone, at the church building, and at this home number. I needed to call her immediately. The tone was not good. I developed a sense of dread and rushed to call her.

Both my parents were in poor health. Mom had had a lot of surgeries recently and Dad had suffered with diabetes and heart problems for the last several years. I picked up the phone and dialed the international number. It seemed like forever before someone picked up the phone at my parents' house. It was not a family member; it was Dennis Simmons, a preacher friend that Dad had grown up with. I was so totally confused by his answering the phone that I asked who it was; he answered with his name and then asked who I was. When I told him it was Ian, he said, "I am so sorry, Ian, the funeral home is here now to pick up the body. Let me get your brother for you."

Before I could find out who had died, he had stepped away from the phone and left to get my brother. Tears ran down my face. My wife froze in her tracks knowing that the news was devastating. Steven (my brother) picked up the phone and said, "Ian, Dad died in his sleep last night."

So there it was. That moment that you never expect will happen had happened. My father was dead, my family distraught, and I was twelve thousand miles away, unable to help in any way. Grief overwhelmed me to the point that

184

my wife had to take the phone and tell Steven that we would call back later. I wept bitterly for the great loss in my life.

But this story is not so much about the loss of my father but of the events that followed that helped me realize that God does care for us.

I spent the rest of Sunday evening trying to get a flight back to Australia. It was the Fourth of July weekend (and vacation time in America) and all the airlines were filled to capacity. No one single airline could get me to Sydney and all the airline ticket prices were exorbitantly high. One airline wanted $7,000 to fly home the next day. Finally, after several hours of arranging, I managed to get a flight from Nashville to Los Angeles Airport on American Airlines and then switch to United Airlines for the international leg to Sydney. It would take twenty-four hours to get there, fourteen and a half of which would be the non-stop leg to Sydney.

I did not sleep. I could not sleep. I cried all night. Emotionally, I was a wreck. Due to the cost of the flights, I would have to travel alone. My family could not travel with me. So I set myself to preparing for the arduous flight made all that much more difficult by my father's death. I questioned if I could make the trip at all.

Romans 8:28—And we know that all things work together for good to them that love God, to them who are the called according to his purpose.

The next day I kissed my family goodbye and set off on the first leg of the flight home to Sydney. The flight from Nashville to Los Angeles is four hours long. I had traveled this route many times, and the distance does not get any shorter each time that you fly it. The hours dragged by; the tears flowed quietly. I prayed for help. I asked God to get me through this difficult time and for his strength to get me the rest of the way home. Even after praying, I felt totally alone. No one around me knew why I was upset; they just left me alone and looked away.

Psalms 142:4—I look to the right and watch, but there is none who takes notice of me; no refuge remains to me, no man cares for me.

After landing at Los Angeles airport, I had three hours to wait for the flight to Sydney. As I checked in, the airline upgraded me to business class, knowing that I had tried to get a bereavement fare home to Australia. Since all the regular economy seats were full, the lady was nice enough to get me into business class. I would have more room; I could stretch out, and try to relax a little. I made my way through security and up to the waiting area for the flight. I walked up to the gate, sat down and prepared myself to face the next three hours prior to the flight leaving. Waves of sadness started to come over me, as I now had nothing to distract me from the sadness of my Dad's passing.

I heard a voice from somewhere in the crowd. It was familiar, but from my past. As I looked up, a familiar face was walking towards me. It was Dale Hartman, a missionary that I had known for the twenty-eight years that he worked with the church in Australia. He walked up, hugged me, and said that he was sorry about my father.

I was amazed that he was here, and that he knew about Dad. He had just been on the phone to his family in Oklahoma and had gotten the news from them that my father had passed away. He turned from that conversation and saw me sitting in the waiting area. He said that he was in economy class on my flight to Sydney, traveling with a new missionary family. He had three hours to kill and wanted to know if he could talk with me about Dad. So he offered to buy me dinner.

Isaiah 40:31—but they who wait for the LORD shall renew their strength, they shall mount up with wings like eagles, they shall run and not be weary, they shall walk and not faint.

In the three hours before our flight, we talked about Dad and how he had been a supporter of Dale's mission work. Dale told me about times when he had left for a teaching session in Australia with only $40 in his pocket for the month that he would be there. He told me about how Dad would secretly offer to take care of his expenses while he was there. He told me things that I never knew my father had done that helped with his mission efforts.

He spoke of the encouragement that Dad had given him and how he had always been there for him. He was a great comfort to me during the time that we were together. As we parted to go and get on the flight, Dale prayed one more time with me and then said he would see me "on the other side of the pond" once we had landed.

Psalms 55:22—Cast your burden on the LORD, and he will sustain you; he will never permit the righteous to be moved.

As I lined up to go through the business class boarding line, I kept hearing the desk page: "Dale Hartman, please come to the check-in counter." After about five pages I had made my way into the plane, sat down in row 7F and prepared myself for the next fourteen-and-a-half lonely hours.

A few moments later, I heard a voice from behind me say "I can't sit next to that man, I have know him for 28 years!" It was Dale. The boarding desk had paged him five times to come up to the counter. The first four times when he went up, they told him that they had not paged him. So he stepped away. The fifth time he was paged, he went up to the desk, the lady took his ticket and tore it up. They needed his seat, she said, and he would be reseated on the plane. That seat was 7G in business class right next to me.

Proverbs 18:24—There are friends who pretend to be friends, but there is a friend who sticks closer than a brother.

Flights leave for Sydney 365 days a year. They leave out of either of the two major west coast airports. There are at least ten flights on four major airlines that leave each day and on each flight as many as five hundred people will crowd onto the plane. Through an incomprehensible chain of events, my prayer had been answered. I had an old friend sitting beside me.

Proverbs 17:17—A friend loves at all times, and a brother is born for adversity.

In the next fourteen-and-a-half hours Dale was there for me as a friend. When I needed to talk, we talked. We prayed together. Dale read to me from the Bible. He read to me from Proverbs. He was able to talk to the flight attendants about the incredible coincidence of our meeting and being seated together. He could articulate the loss that I had experienced to those attendants so they understood the stress that I was under. He was the comfort that I needed in the hour of trial.

Galatians 6:2—Bear one another's burdens, and so fulfill the law of Christ

To this day; I get chills up and down my spine to think of the series of coincidences that led us to be together that night. We were two Christians traveling to the other side of the world—one needing a friend, one being that friend. I had prayed for help to get me through a difficult situation, and, through the providence of God, that prayer was answered.

Psalms 94:19—When the cares of my heart are many, thy consolations cheer my soul.

So what have I learned from this experience?

1. There are some things that you just can't explain.

2. You are never asked to bear more than you are able.

3. Christian friendships are timeless.

4. God will find a way.

5. Never underestimate the power of prayer.

6. Be careful what you pray for; you just might get it.

Life Lesson Number 505

—

"He is Heavy, He's my Father"

My Dad was a big man. When I say big, I mean "big." I take after him and as they say, "The apple doesn't fall far from the tree." Now I was not there for this part of Dad's story, but my brother and brother-in-law (both big brawny fellows themselves) told me what happened.

After Mum had found that Dad had died in his sleep, she called my brother Steven to come over immediately.

Steve, of course, rushed over to be with Mum in a house filled with police officers, paramedics, doctors, preachers and family friends. He also needed to be there to help make arrangements.

Dad had a history of heart problems, so his doctor had been able to write a "Cause of Death" certificate immediately. After the police and medical personnel had left, Steve found himself alone with Mark (our brother-in-law). Steve had worked with Dad many times on putting together funeral arrangements, and Dad had instructed him exactly what should be done when it was his turn to "fall off the perch."

Steve dutifully called the funeral home that Dad had selected and told them that they needed to come pick up Dad's body from the family home in Blacktown. Before finalizing the arrangements to pick up Dad, Steve tried to jog the memory of the funeral home attendant by saying, "You do remember Dad, don't you? He was a big man." Steve waited for the penny to drop about "how big Dad was" with the attendant, but it did not. So Steve tried a less subtle method by suggesting that they might need someone skilled in the arts of moving "large bodies" from house to vehicle. Apparently, Steve got some indication that they would take care of this.

About thirty minutes later the funeral home van pulls up to the house. A knock on the front door reveals that the funeral home had sent a petite eighteen-year-old girl (who weighed about 110 pounds ringing wet) and what appeared to be a wizened emphasemic 80-year-old man who was barely able to carry the body bag up the front steps. When Steve saw this dynamic duo, I can imagine his thought process ("This is not my problem. Just step out of the way and let them take care of it"). This he does; he stands aside, and watches, along with Mark and Dennis Simmons (Dad's best friend), as the duo head up the hall to the death-bed.

Apparently there was a long pause when the two entered the room. No noise, no movement, their faces frozen or perhaps stunned (like a kangaroo or deer stuck in the headlights of a car). After a few whispers, both reappear down the hallway. The old gentlemen clears his throat and says, "Look, he appears to be a pretty big fellow, and there is no way the two of us can get him off the bed, into the bag, down the hall, and into the van. I think we might have to get the coppers or medics to come back and give us a bit of a hand!"

Steven looked over at Mark and Dennis, rolled his eyes, and said, "Don't worry about it, mate! We'll take care of it." So up the hall goes son Steven, son-in-law Mark, and friend Dennis.

Now, Dad was a "big man," but the room was quite small where he died. So the boys had a bit of a logistical problem ahead of them. After laying out the open body bag, and positioning themselves around Dad's body, they heaved Dad onto the floor, positioned his arms, zipped the bag closed and took a breather (rest). (Remember, Dad was a "very big man.")

Now obviously the shortest distance between two points is a straight line. In this case, that would have been out the bedroom door, down the hall, out the front door, down a flight of about fifteen steps and into the van. I can see the worried look on Steve's and Mark's faces as they realized what might happen. Two right turns and two left turns followed by a hasty descent down a staircase with no railing, all the while trying to control mass and acceleration (remember that old $E=MC^2$). After a hasty conference, it was decided to take the more circuitous route, which gave them a gentle descent to the van at the side of the house. This involved traversing the length of the whole house, negotiating turns around all the furniture, crossing the porch, and finagling the gentle slope of the walkway down to the van—four times the distance of the first route, but much safer.

With the route decided, they set off. Dennis on the top right corner and Steve on the top left, Mark on the bottom right, and the dynamic duo both trying to keep their one corner up off the ground. I never did find out how many times they had to stop on the way out to the van. Never-the-less, they finally made it and got Dad situated where they could get him to the funeral home. It was the dead of winter but the boys were sweating profusely. As Steve closed the doors to the van, I can see him wondering how they would get Dad out at the other end. It was not his problem.

As the time for Dad's funeral approached, I made my trek from overseas and found out some more details about Dad's funeral. Apparently, when Sue and Steve went to pick out his coffin the funeral home mentioned that they might need a "Special Custom Made Coffin" for Dad. Sue and Steve nodded knowingly at this, and of course Steve (as directed by Dad) stated: "Of course, there is no extra charge for that, is there?" It turns out that there was no extra charge. Dad would have been pleased.

By now the funeral home knew how big Dad was. They had ordered him a custom made extra large (robust) coffin and we were ready to go. The morning of the funeral, it struck us that we should call the gravediggers and make sure that they knew how big Dad was. There is nothing worse than going to a funeral where the coffin jams in the hole causing great consternation as the coffin is retrieved and the shovels come out to clean up what should have been done right in the first place. The gravediggers knew Dad, knew how big he was, and guaranteed us that there was no way "Cliffy" was going to hang up. They would take care of it, and they did.

When we arrived at the graveside for Dad's service, I got to see him for one last time. I was a little bit concerned that they might have made him a bubble top or doublewide coffin that looked embarrassing for all concerned. I was wrong; the coffin was uniformly large and not disproportionate in any way. Steve and Sue had done a wonderful job in picking such a wonderful color and style.

Dad's coffin was about twenty feet away from his grave and it was located on a small table that held it at about waist height off the ground. Steve, Mark and I were to be pallbearers along with three of Dad's nephews. There were six of us, none of us under two hundred pounds and a few of us over three hundred. (Ok, one I know was maybe close to four hundred pounds). A hefty bunch of brawny boys (to say the least) set upon the task of getting Uncle/Dad to the grave.

When the time came to get the coffin to the grave, Steve and I gravitate to the head. Why, I don't know. In hindsight, it was a bad move. I did at least have the forethought of putting Steve on the left side of the coffin where he would have to step over the great cavernous hole. If the soil gave way, there was no way I was going to be on the bottom if we were all going in. (Isn't brotherly love a wonderful thing?)

We stepped beside the coffin, grabbed the handle, and then tried to stand up straight. Now, I say tried and I mean tried. Remember, Dad was a "big" man. Add to that, the weight of a "special" coffin and we're talking five to maybe six hundred pounds of literal dead weight.

With 200 to 250 people looking on, we eyed each other, gritted our teeth, and then heaved Dad off the coffin holder. Each and every step we took towards that grave became harder. I started to quiver, literally (like one of those overweight weight lifters at the Olympics as they try to heave large weights over their head). I tried to indicate to the other guys that I needed to take a breather, and that we should put him down half way. I got a look of concern from Steven and understood that he was in the same condition I was. I could tell that Steve is thinking, "If we put him down now, I will never get him back up again!" The thoughts of attending a funeral where the first "Tag-Team Pallbearers" would have to be used appalled us both, so we struggled on.

Having made it to the grave, and not fallen in, we put Dad down next to the lowering device. We stood upright, stretched our backs, and then were given instructions on how we were to move the coffin over the lowering device. "Oh great" I think to myself, "we have to lift again."

It turned out to be more of a slide than a lift. So Steve throws one leg over the other side of the extra wide grave, grabs the handle and we try to slide. Now the boys at the other end (where the feet are) have their end whipped over in a moment. I could see the look of relief on their faces as they stepped away from their completed duties. It was left to Steve, Mark and me to get Dad all lined up for the final lowering. With one final heave Dad moved into position. A great weight came off my mind; however, a great weigh suddenly hit the lowering device.

It took a few moments to realize what was happening. People stared in amazement. There were a few oh's and ah's from the crowd as they saw what was happening. Finally, the funeral director rushes in to save the day. As we put the full weight of Dad on the lowering device, the braking system started to fail. Dad slowly started to disappear into the hole. Were it not for the fleet-footed funeral director knocking me out of the way, jumping on the foot brake, and locking down the lowering device it would have all been over. Dad stopped, the bottom half of his coffin in the grave, the top half out. We apprehensively stood back and waited for the service to begin. We winced every time we heard the braking device groan.

It was a lovely service. The coffin stayed where it was supposed to, and lowered with space to spare into the extra large hole Dad's gravedigger friends had prepared for him.

Afterward, as everybody left, Steven, Mark and I stayed behind. I had suggested that we should fill Dad's grave in, both as a sign of respect for what he was to us, and to give us a sense of closure. As we stood around and shoveled dirt into Dad's grave, we struck up a conversation with the funeral director. We commented on how lovely the coffin was and how well proportioned it was.

The director said, "Yes, it was a nice coffin. You know, we had to measure him up for it. It was 22 inches deep through. But you know what: when we put him in and crossed his hands on his chest we still couldn't get the lid on!" Steve and I looked at each other and smiled. He went on, "We had to stand him at attention and move his radio [that's a whole other story] out of his pocket to get the lid on!" We told the director not to worry. Dad had been in the army and didn't mind standing at attention for eternity.

So what have I learned from this experience?

1. Dad had a sense of humor about everything, even death. I can see him, shoulders slumped, head bowed forward, laughing over the discomfort his size caused.

2. The strangest things in life can bind brothers and brothers-in-law together. Some memories are priceless.

3. Self-preservation and the fear of "great huge holes" sometimes override the need to show brotherly love.

4. Appearance (stately movement to the grave) and reality (not going to make it, not going to make it!) are two different things.

5. Go for the feet first, even if you have to knock people down.

6. Never send an eighteen-year-old girl and an eighty-year-old guy to do five people's work.

7. When we say "big" we mean "BIG."

8. There may be a future for tag team pall-bearing.

Life Lesson Number 510

—

"What if?"

It struck me the other day that life can be so short and so unpredictable. When Dad died I began to reevaluate my own life and to take stock of who I was, where I was going, and how good a father I had been to Tabitha and Ethan. It was during this process that I realized that I had two very young and special children who still had a lot of developing and growing left to do. I felt that my work with them was quite unfinished.

I asked myself the question, "What if I were not here to guide and help them through their lives?" Other than our life experiences together up to this point, do they have a roadmap of thoughts and expectations that they could use to remind them of what was important and of what I wanted for them in their lives? I felt that the answer to that question was no. I needed to give them some thoughts, wishes, expectations and hopes that might help them focus on what should be important in their lives.

While thinking of what I could do for Tabitha and Ethan, I remembered that I had heard two wonderful family therapists (Brecheen and Faulkner) who recommended that a father should have a special prayer or blessing for his children. Its basis comes from the blessings given by the patriarchs in the Old Testament and it provides a powerful message for the child, one that they will always have and remember as they live the lives we wish for them.

So it was that I set out to prepare these prayers for my children. In each case I wanted to express what I felt were the beautiful personality traits that I saw in each child and then I moved on to my hopes for our eternal future together.

These were difficult prayers to write as they dealt with hopes and expectations that would go on after I had left this world. I decided that there could be no more personal a gift from a father to a child than the thoughts that were expressed in the following prayers.

A Father's Blessing—For Tabitha

Dearest Heavenly Father

I thank you for my daughter, Tabitha,
For the joy she brings to my heart,
For her love of what is right and just,
For the love she has for you,
For the good choices that she makes in life

I thank you for her love of learning,
For the joy she finds in music and literature,
For her quick mind and good humor,
For her free and adventurous spirit,
For the Christian beauty that she is

I thank you for her mischievous smile,
For her angelic face,
For her golden strands of hair,
For her deepest blue eyes,
For her soft and caring hands

She refreshes my soul

I pray that you will be with her all the days of
her life,
Help her to always put you first,
Create in her a desire to spread your word,
Help her to make good choices when facing
difficult decisions,
And to choose the narrow pathway

Bless her with a good husband,
One that will help her get to heaven,
Help her to love and cherish her family,
Keep her safe from all evil

I ask that you grant her a long and prosperous life,
May her children marvel at her faithfulness to you,
May her grandchildren call her blessed,
May her great grandchildren learn your ways from her example,

And when her time comes to be gathered to her reward,
May she approach your throne with your Son at her side,
Being found faithful in all things,
And let us all again be joined in an unbroken circle,
Worshipping at your throne

This is my prayer for Tabitha, In Jesus Name, Amen

A Father's Blessing—For Ethan

Dearest Heavenly Father

I thank you for my son, Ethan
For the joy he brings to my life,
For his love of what is right and just,
For his kind and gentle heart,
For the love he has for your word

I thank you for his boundless energy,
For his competitive spirit,
For the close relationship that we have,
For his quick wit and good humor,
For the honor and integrity he exudes,
For the Christian man that he is

I thank you for his tender heart,
For his compassionate soul,
For his warming smile,
For his deep blue eyes,
For his strong and caring hands

He refreshes my hopes for the future

I pray that you will be with him all the days of his life,
Help him to always put you first,
Create in him a desire to spread your word,
Help him to make good choices when facing difficult decisions,
And to choose the narrow pathway

Bless him with a good wife,
One that will help him get to heaven,
Help him to love and cherish his family,
Keep him safe from all evil
I ask that you grant him a long and prosperous life,
May his faith be found strong in his children,
May his Christian example lead his grandchildren to righteousness,
May his great grandchildren study your word at his side

And when his time comes to be gathered to his reward,
May he approach your throne with your Son at his side,
Being found faithful in all things,
And let us all again be joined in an unbroken circle,
Worshipping at your throne

This is my prayer for Ethan, In Jesus Name, Amen

◆   ◆   ◆

Each child has a framed copy of these words superimposed over their pictures in their bedrooms. I have the same copies in my office at work. I see these pictures each and every day and I pray these words each and every day. They are a powerful reminder of the responsibility I bear as a parent.

So what have I learned from this experience?

1. Take time to think about your children's future in terms other than success and riches.

2. Ask yourself if your loved ones really know how you feel about them.

3. The process of preparing the prayer will change your own priorities in life.

4. Draw on your own parent's unwritten hopes and expectations to help you navigate life's trials and tribulations.

5. Pray for your children every day.

Life Lesson Number 520

—

"You're going to snake that WHERE?"

When you finally pass the ripe old age of forty, you begin to accept certain things about visits to the doctors. Guys, you know what I am talking about. It's that wonderful hands on experience that we all have to deal with in those post-forty yearly checkups. You walk in the door to the exam room and the nurse asks you how you're doing and then after some small talk she sets out everything that the doctor will need to complete his examination. Without any thought to your mental state, she slams down a rubber glove and the KY jelly. Oh, she knew what she was doing when she did it. It is a woman's one chance to get back at all men for what they have to experience at their own doctor's visit.

As I sat there for what seemed like hours, looking at the glove and the jelly, it struck me that I should be thankful for what was about to happen to me. I had recently been thinking about a disturbing trend in medicine that when looked at in individual occurrences meant nothing, but when strung together indicated to me a conspiracy so deep and dark that it overshadowed both the "Area 51 cover ups" and "Kennedy's assassination conspiracy." People, I am talking of a conspiracy worse than any covert black helicopters from the UN and men in black visiting your home. Let me bring you up to speed on where I am.

Over the years I have had many types of "procedures" that were prescribed by the doctors who treated me. It all started innocently enough with the Ear, Nose and Throat specialist snaking a tube up my nose to check out my sinuses. But things progressed from there to a whole new level. I had knee surgery a few years later where the orthopedic surgeon cut a few small holes in my knee, snaked in a tube and performed miraculous surgery on a knee that I thought would never work again. The same thing happened when I had a bad appendicitis attack. The abdominal surgeon cut three small holes in my stomach and removed all sorts of wonderful things after snaking that black tube inside me.

Of course the trend didn't stop there. Sometimes the surgeons didn't have to cut. They just found orifices that would accommodate the long black snaking tube and set to resolving my problems through these ready-made manholes. I had a stomachache, so what did they do? They snaked a tube down into my stomach and did some procedure that made me feel better. Another time I had a belly ache, so they snaked another tube up the other way to see what was happening. One day I developed a kidney stone and guess what? They snaked the same size tube up the front passage and dragged that little puppy out. Throughout all these "snakings," it did not strike me as odd what was going on, but today it did.

In recent years these doctors have decided that they no longer want to touch their patients. So they spend inordinate amounts of time putting together these complex snake machines that can do everything from fill you full of air to sealing you shut with the twist of some Edward-Scissor-Hands-like hand device, and all this from a distance of three feet. Through all these procedures they keep you awake so that you will become comfortable with this hands-off approach. Why, you might ask, have they developed these new devices? They have dark and sinister forces driving them, that's why.

Can't you see who is behind all this? Listen to me closely and I will tell you. "The Professional Golfers Association" is behind all this. The medical and golf associations have gotten together in one of the blackest operations known to modern man. It is my understanding that doctors would rather play golf all day than do anything else. The PGA knows this. But what hinders these doctors from golfing all day? That's right, those troublesome patients! But what if the doctors could treat their patients without actually being "with" their patients? Can you see where I am going with this?

If a doctor can stand three feet away from you and operate on every conceivable part of your anatomy through a half inch black tube while working Edward Scissor Hand knobs why does he have to be just three feet away? It is my understanding that the PGA and Medical associations have been plowing millions of dollars into remote access surgery. That's right, people. Surgery over the web is the next logical step. Three feet, thirty miles or three hundred miles will make no difference.

The surgeons have mastered the skills and procedures and the lowly paid nurses have been trained to insert the tubes. It is my understanding that the PGA has actually designed a golf cart with a remote access PC and Edwards Scissor Hands controls so that these guys can golf all day, and operate between putts.

I can see the cell phone conversations now! "Hello honey, what? No! I am on the seventh green. I need to putt out before Frank, remove a polyp from Mr. Shepherd's colon, and head on out to the eighth tee. I should be home after golf and Mr. Barker's appendectomy."

Now some of you may be asking yourself this question, "What is wrong with letting these doctors operate remotely? Three feet or thirty miles should make no difference." Let me explain to you my reasoning for being adamantly against this practice. It all comes down to one thing, and one thing only.

Bored five-year-olds.

Why should we be concerned with bored five-year-olds you might ask?

I say we should be concerned because I was one and I know what they are capable of!

My greatest fear is that somewhere out there in cyberspace a bored web-enabled five-year-old will reprogram his XBox, drop onto the web, and hijack my next colonoscopy. That is why I am against the whole thing!

I can see the startled look on the surgeon's face as his remote golf cart screen goes blank, and I can see little Timmy smiling as he takes over what appears to be a really cool game of Doom or Tomb Raider. Timmy's mother calls out to him and tells him to come down for dinner and he yells back that he can't because he has to laser slam the bad polyp people, suck out the brown slimers, create a wind tunnel with his blower, and then find a few secret doors and extra secret tunnels. The horror! No wait! It is the ultimate horror—that my colon be featured as the next must-have video game for kiddies.

So I sit here in the waiting room staring at the rubber glove and KY jelly and, you know what, I am thankful that my doctor has not fallen prey to the dark side of his profession. Today, I am the lucky one. I am getting a little one-on-one with my doctor and I for once will not complain about the personal touch.

<u>*So what have I learned from this experience?*</u>

1. Just say no to "snaking."

2. Always question if they wiped off the snake after their last colonoscopy.

3. When checking out a new doctor, ask what his handicap is before you decide on choosing him.

4. When you see an up-linked golf cart on a green with some guy working Edward Scissor Hand controls, don't sneak up and say boo! You could hurt someone.

5. We really do need to find more stuff for bored five-year-olds to do!

6. If you look hard enough, there can be a bright side to everything. Okay, sometimes you have to look "really, really hard."

Life Lesson Number 530

—

"Death by Taxi"

Having the active mind that I do, it took me all of fifteen minutes to figure out why 98% of Mexican citizens are die-hard Catholics. It was a simple deduction really and anyone can figure it out for himself. All you have to do is take a taxi ride anywhere in Mexico and the answer is obvious.

I leaned out to beckon one of the green and white taxis in Monterrey over to the curb. As the small green rocket approached at great speed (while crossing three lanes of traffic accompanied by the cacophony of horns, screeching brakes, and wild arm gestures), I made my first observation. The word "Size" registered in my mind as the Geo Metro screeched to a halt in front of me. I indicated for my wife and two children to squeeze into the back seat and then attempted to maneuver my large frame into the front seat next to the driver. I am a big man. This was a small car. How small you might ask? Let me just say this: "I did not get into the car, I put it on!"

After two attempts at closing the door to seal in my hugeness, we were finally ready to be off on our little trip. My wife gave the instructions to the cab driver and smoke burned from the front tires as we pulled out from the curb attempting to break some quarter-mile speed record. A quick look over my shoulder told me that my wife and kids were already bug-eyed at the driver's antics. When I turned back around, I noticed another interesting thing about this pocket rocket that had slipped by my usually attentive observation skills. Bolted to the hood of the car was an eight-inch bright blue statue of the Virgin Mary.

Scanning my eyes back further, I also noticed that the rear vision mirror was so full of hanging religious icons that the driver had resorted to suction cups across the front windscreen to dangle these much needed driving diversions. I counted seven different dangling icons all swaying freely and blocking a good 50% of the visible windscreen area. As best I could tell, we had all the saints covered. Not knowing the names of the specific saints didn't really matter, because I figured somewhere in this protective grouping was the "blessed mother of acceleration", obviously one of this driver's favorites.

My first thought was, "Saints: this might be a good thing?" thinking that we were in some sort of religious protection program that the driver had instigated. But then, after watching the antics of the driver for a few moments, I realized that these icons were there to comfort us prior to the moment of our impending death.

As we careened down the street, I noticed that not only did the driver have the religious icons all over the front of the car, but he was also holding a rosary in his right hand, flicking through it feverishly as we cut from lane to lane, mouthing some secret prayer, and all the while changing gears with that right hand, doing the sign of the cross and gesturing out the left window with the other hand. It was a marvel of coordination. I was giddy with the sheer effort being put forth and the frenzy of his gesticulations.

I looked at the driver's taxi registration card and noticed that his first name was "Jesus." After I read that special piece of information, the question did go through my mind as to why would Jesus be driving a cab in Mexico and when did he change his last name to Fernandez and profession to taxi driver, but I digress. Obviously our driver was a religious man.

I could go into gruesome detail of what our trip involved but thought it best to summarize and leave it to your imagination as to how it really felt. Needless to say, add to this list of experiences a cold clammy sweat, bug-eyed incredulity, hushed screams of horror, and much white-knuckle dashboard holding, and you will get the picture.

1. Running red lights—which apparently are only suggestions that you may need to stop.

2. Driving down the wrong side of the road and making your own turn lane—lines painted on the roads are only suggestions. Lines, we don't need no stinking lines!

3. Driving the wrong way up a one way street—remember signs are just suggestions, no one really follows what they say.

4. Pedestrian Crossings—Oh look, Juan is trying to make it to the other side! Open season on pedestrians if you ask me.

5. Speed Bumps—merely a challenge to see how much ground clearance and distance you can gain before crashing back to earth.

6. Sidewalks—places free of traffic and places to pass tight traffic jams at high speed.

7. Pedestrians—merely mobile speed bumps.

8. Turn indicators—on the odd occasion that they are used they mean that either "I might do something in the future" or "I may have done something in the past" that required your attention.

9. Speeding—130 KPH in a 40 KPH zone. Speed appeared to be relative to the number of police in sight.

    a. No police—go fast.

    b. Some police—go fast.

    c. Many police—go fast.

    (Actually, speed was relative to your chances of being pursued and caught. I can see this guy thinking, "Those coppers will never catch me in this traffic!")

10. Speed was also relative to the distance required to stop. Otherwise, it was foot flat to the floor the whole time.

Having made it through the somewhat busy part of town where three lanes actually contained five rows of cars, we came to an open part of a two-lane road. Finding ourselves stuck behind a car doing only 80 KPH in a 40KPH zone (obviously much too slow), the driver decided to pass over double yellow lines going up the crest of a hill. Having committed to the passing maneuver, we were greeted at the crest of the hill with an 18-wheeler barreling down on us, lights blazing, and horns blaring.

At this particular moment I found out that I had a talent that prior to this special occasion I had not known about. I had no airbag, and I had no seatbelt; what could possibly save me from certain death? It was then that I realized that my bottom cheeks had clenched and actually grabbed foam in the seat where I was sitting. I had anchored myself ready for impact. As I closed my eyes waiting for the certain impact to occur, I could see the rescue squad having to get out the Jaws of

Life to cut through the foam fabric of the seat and release my lifeless body from its anchor point. I almost smiled at that little vision of loveliness.

Through some miracle we made it back onto the right side of the road without impacting the front of the truck. It was then that I noticed that I too had begun to frantically make the sign of the cross. So that was it! I had stumbled on yet another major world conspiracy. I am sure that the Pope has given direct instructions to all Taxi drivers in Mexico that people may enter their cabs as heathens but when and if they leave, they should all be good Catholics.

So what have I learned from this experience?

1. In Mexico, if you don't have religion when you get into the cab, you will have it when you leave.

2. Your anatomy can learn to do new and wondrous things.

3. In Mexico, if you do get into a cab and it has more than three religious icons accompanied by a recorded message telling you to "Please hold on to the bar," back out quickly and leave.

4. In Mexico, if the driver throws back his head, laughs and screams, "Rules, we don't need no stinking rules!", you're definitely in trouble.

5. I have decided that we have been doing it all wrong in trying to convert people to our church. We are way too subtle. We must threaten converts with imminent physical death.

6. Our church should be training taxi drivers, not missionaries!

7. In our church taxi service, we would need a failed water jump attempt at the end to get people saved.

8. Some of the other churches might just need a drive-through car wash.

9. A certain Old Testament religion might only need to cut three inches off the exhaust pipe of the taxi at the end of each run.

Life Lesson Number 535

—

"Anarchy"

It happened while my husband worked out-of-state through the week and returned home on weekends:

So there I am, sitting on my queenly throne (the recliner), commanding my royal subjects (my family) to do my bidding...

"Tabitha, you need to practice your clarinet!" I yell (in a queenly way, of course) to my thirteen-year-old daughter.

"Ethan, put the dishes in the dishwasher!" I bellow (in a most royal tone) to my eleven-year-old son.

"Ian, may I have some coffee?" I condescend to the most loyal of my subjects (aka "my husband").

They stop...Stillness...Then...Inklings of anarchy?

"Boy, she's bossy," states the most loyal of my subjects, my husband, to his comrade-in-gender.

"You think that's bad..." I await with baited breath the ungrateful boy's eleven-year-old response, "You're lucky you're only here two days a week. I've got to put up with her twenty four by seven!"

My reign, as we know it, has come to an end.........

Queen Dee Ann

So what have I learned from this experience?

1.   No matter how benevolent the reign, the natives are always restless.

2.   Even the king can be swayed.

3.   The court jester should always mind his mother.

Life Lesson Number 536

—

"Stinky Stuff"

We had an unexpected visitor at our house yesterday (Sunday). We woke up on Sunday morning to the smell of skunk wafting through the house (it brought back memories of our skunk-ridden time in Clyde, TX). I was sure a skunk had gotten under the house. Not sure how. Must have been a kamikaze skunk to make its way through three dogs. We had to hurry off to church, so couldn't check on it.

When we got home in the afternoon, Tabitha looked out the window and yelled, "There's a dead skunk in our backyard!" Sure enough, the kamikaze skunk was now a dead skunk. (That'll teach it to mess with MY dogs!)

An exciting afternoon was had by all.........scooping up the dead skunk while fending off the smelly dogs and burying it in the field behind our house. It wasn't foaming at the mouth, so the "experts" at Animal Control told us it "probably didn't have rabies and died of natural causes." Yeah, three really big, annoying, and now stinky natural causes named Lucy, Emmy Lou, and Pacer!!!!!

There's probably a moral to this story, but I can't think and hold my nose at the same time, so it will have to wait.

One wonders what was going through the skunk's mind (besides the dogs' teeth, of course). Who knows? Who cares? All I know is that that was one really DUMB skunk.

Love,

Queen Dee Ann

<u>*So what have I learned from this experience?*</u>

1. Kamikaze skunks? Perhaps a plot to take over our backyard?

2. Our dufus dogs don't know the difference between playing and killing.

3. Natural causes? Apparently any death other than by bullet wound.

Life Lesson Number 537

—

"The Heart"

He wandered around appearing to aimlessly fiddle with some left over pipe cleaners that we were using to make a science project. He hugged me as I said goodbye to him for the week and he went to get in the other car to go to Bible bowl. As I got into my car, there it was—a pipe cleaner heart sitting between the seats.

I looked at him, picked up the heart, put it in my pocket, patted it and waved as he smiled at me and drove off with tears in his eyes. I too was moved to tears by this simple loving act.

So what have I learned from this experience?

1. Sometimes the simplest of things can say, "I love you and miss you."

2. A son needs a father as much as a father needs a son.

Life Lesson Number 538

—

"The Call"

I was fifteen miles north of Birmingham, Alabama, on my way back to my apartment in Montgomery. The new job necessitated that we be apart through the week. My cell phone rang and it was my son Ethan. He was so excited that he just had to call and tell me that he had led not one, but two, songs at the singing night at our church in Florence.

I had missed it. This stretch that he had made to overcome his fear of people. My heart swelled with pride at the choice he made and yet hurt that I was not there to see him victorious over his fears.

So what have I learned from this experience?

1. Sometimes a father has to do hard things to keep the family fed.

2. A son can step in for his father and fill his shoes when he is away.

3. You can face your fears and win.

Life Lesson Number 539

—

"The Band"

She ran into the room yelling at the top of her voice. She could not contain her excitement at having made it into the Mid State Band. She had beaten out three hundred other clarinet players to make First Band, Fouth chair in the Tennessee Mid State Band. No other student at her school had beaten so many and placed so highly in the tough competition. We cried as we hugged each other.

I realized for the first time that my little girl Tabitha has found her passion in life and is pursuing it with all her might. She loves her music and how it makes her feel. I love the fact that she has found her identity and is pursuing her dream.

So what have I learned from this experience?

1. Help your children develop, seek and follow their dreams.

2. Support your child's goals even if they are not exactly what you planned for them.

Life Lesson Number 539

—

"The Summary"

For those of us who find it hard to pay attention, I thought it might be good just to summarize the lessons that I learned in these few stories presented in this book. So pay attention this time; it might save you some grief and embarrassment if you remember these few life lessons.

So what have I learned from this experience?

1. The combination of the names "Percy" and "Pickles" has an interesting effect on old ladies.

2. When a three-year-old tells you he needs to go to the toilet now, he really means NOW!

3. Sugar Doodles and Fast Trains should never be combined.

4. Always keep a good handkerchief handy. You never know when you might need it.

5. The Daddy's prayer does not always work.

6. If you ever find yourself in a really crowded train and you want to get a good seat, then…nah! Who am I kidding? That would be too horrible a thought.

7. Dads, if you throw the "selfish/self-centered card" early in the game, don't expect Mum to throw the "Oh, let me help you out of this embarrassing situation" card when you need it.

8. If you steal your grandfather's chocolate coconut balls, you get into big trouble.

9. You can get your mouth washed out with soap for doing things other than saying bad words.

10. Stay inside on mowing day. Grandfathers get grumpy if they have to go back to push mowing the lawn.

11. Even a three-year-old gets tired of lamb chops after a few weeks.

12. No matter how hard you look, sometimes you never find where grandfather hides his chocolate coconut ball stash.

13. Fire is "Bad!"

14. Boys who play with fire are "Bad!"

15. The distance a five-year-old can carry a flaming roll of paper is inversely proportional to the size of the flame.

16. All cigarette lighters are not child proof.

17. Hessian flares up like wafer thin toilet paper when exposed to an open flame.

18. Grandfathers are grumpy when they are not allowed to smoke anymore.

19. Catholic girls have no sense of humor.

20. Fences don't always make for good neighbors; in fact they hardly slow their kids down.

21. Choosing the right target is more important than hitting the target.

22. Timing is everything when it comes to your escape plan.

23. You can literally get the snot beat out of you.

24. Catholic girls are mean, but they scare easy.

25. Fences sure do slow down old people who are chasing you.

26. Five-year-olds innately have the feral ability to scale fences of any height.

27. Always remove rolled up newspapers from the sidewalk before you do something stupid.

28. Never assume that you will MISS something that you are aiming for.

29. Hiding under the bed each time the dry cleaning man makes a delivery is hard to explain to your Nana.

30. With a little work you can "join wicks together" to give you more time to escape.

31. Explosives and young boys should be closely supervised.

32. Dog poop can travel at twice the speed of a seven-year-old.

33. It takes three days before your mother smells the clothes hidden under your mattress.

34. Always, I repeat, always keep your mouth closed in disposal operations like this.

35. Cats don't like me.

36. After this incident, you never could find string at Grandmother's house.

37. Cats don't like scuba diving in the bathtub.

38. Cats can't play soccer.

39. Cats don't like dogs.

40. You can't stuff a round cat into a square hole.

41. You can parachute a cat into a pack of wild dogs, but the cat really doesn't like it.

42. Grandmothers are the most patient people in the world.

43. Cats do have nine lives. They just use them up quicker around me.

44. Give me a roll of duct tape, a Leatherman tool, three snickers, and ten bored five-year-olds and I could take over a small country.

45. Grandmothers never tell your parents the really bad things that you do.

46. Conservation of energy comes naturally to farmers. "Yeah sure, we could dig a big hole…but…that would be work!"

47. When it comes to digging dirt, the smaller the hole and sharper the axe the better.

48. Mothers sometimes don't think outside the box.

49. Fathers just want to stuff the box full and bury it.

50. I wonder if Mother ever worried about growing old and feeble with a man who could shoot, dismember, and bury a lifelong friend the moment it got sick.

51. Check the boot (trunk) of the car for "burying" tools if Dad ever offers to take you to the doctor.

52. Never let it be said that my Dad COULD NOT put a square plug in a round hole. He would just shave off the sides and make it fit.

53. Always listen closely in church.

54. Never assume that you heard what you think you heard.

55. Never assume that what you said was what was heard.

56. A stigma can be attached to your person without you even being present, and it can last for a lifetime. Wait, it has actually lasted past Mabel's lifetime.

57. I have figured out the brown spot thing, but I have no idea what a dummy tit is?

58. When you're dead, you're dead.

59. There are no degrees of death.

60. Death rituals should be carefully explained to small children.

61. Regardless of what Nana tells you, there is no such thing as "looking natural" when you're dead. You just look dead.

62. When you get that first pension check, cash it quickly.

63. Being good and working hard doesn't guarantee a long life.

64. You should always hide the kewpie doll stick if you're going to be bad.

65. You should never wait thirty years to tell the truth about something you did.

66. Just being able to "see someone" will not keep her alive. It just makes you feel better.

67. Never assume that your child will only throw up ONCE and then get over it.

68. Never leave a bored child in a complex piece of machinery.

69. Save the roof of your car. Strap your kids down.

70. Never assume that a child will ever understand the word "Stay."

71. Clutch, what's a clutch? I don't need no stinking clutch!

72. The Whip! Not just something you do when water-skiing or while playing Roller Game.

73. Teach your kids to lip read. It might save your life someday.

74. Never double, triple-dare a grandfather, because he will call your bluff.

75. Keep your legs together when you jump from great heights.

76. Grandfathers only think they can act like teenagers.

77. Oxygen is a wonderful thing.

78. When you swim along the shore, watch where you're going.

79. Never, ever, ever jump into water from a great height at low tide. You may hit the bottom of the ocean.

80. To this day I can still see the reflected water patterns from my near-drowning day when I close my eyes in bright sunlight.

81. Lumps on the back of your grandfather's neck make him (shall we say) a little testy.

82. When you think things can't get much worse, they will.

83. You can drown in three inches of water.

84. You can drown on top of a hill.

85. I didn't know it then, but this is one of my first "Hey ya'll watch this" moments.

86. Never expect your friends to get you out of trouble when you have just given them a hard time.

87. You will not die if you sit in wet clothes for three hours. Your mother just thinks you will.

88. I find it hard to watch cricket to this day because of flashbacks.

89. The only thing worse than being "the kid that nearly drowned in three inches of water on the top of a hill" is being "the naked kid with his underwear blowing in the breeze that nearly drowned in three inches of water on the top of a hill."

90. Whenever I feel bad about my own job, I remember what poor old Dan Dan the Dunny Man had to do.

91. Always wash your hands before you eat. Even if you wear gloves.

92. We need to take more time to appreciate what others do for us.

93. Sometimes it is better not to take the shortcut to our goal.

94. Never say you will never do anything, because invariably you find yourself doing it.

95. These fathers put aside personal pride and did what they needed to do to take care of their families financially.

96. Active imaginations can run away from you given a few small facts.

97. Preachers can paint images that will stay with you for a lifetime.

98. You should always question whether you're ready to make the big trip at any time.

99. Car horns can be misinterpreted as trumpets.

100. A beautiful sunrise and an earthquake do not make for the second coming.

101. Learn to ride horses early in life and it might save your life later.

102. When buying toilet seats, don't get the flimsy cheap ones. Go for something a little sturdier.

103. Only a true friend will put Band-Aids on your injured bottom.

104. A father should never break eye contact with his child during the discipline process.

105. If you must run, have an escape plan! You can't think straight when it's all "elbows and knees" to get out of the way.

106. Clean out your closet and underneath your bed regularly. You never know when you might need to hide there.

107. Remember that if you run, you eventually have to come home.

108. Age, belt skills, and patience will overcome youth, stupidity, and speed any day.

109. Don't rely on your neighbors to side with you. They take the side of the parent every time.

110. This is the only belting with Dad's strap that I can remember. I know I had others, but I can't even remember them.

111. Timing is everything.

112. Never assume that you know what is around the next corner.

113. Always wear a belt.

114. What Mother didn't say and what she did gave us years of stories at the dinner table.

115. Actions speak louder than words.

116. Fathers should never break eye contact with their children during the discipline process, even in jest.

117. A father and son can bond over the strangest things in their lives.

118. The Military should probably study the minds of bored eleven-year-olds to improve their own Psychological Operations programs.

119. Nighttime Billy kidnapping raids can be fun for half the family.

120. You can stuff a foam-filled cloth Squirrel into your father's shoe and people won't find it for days.

121. Five-year-olds do not comprehend the circulatory system of a foam Squirrel's foot.

122. You can try to shave a "Billy the koala," but his fur won't grow back.

123. From a five-year-old's perspective, you can be "pegged to death."

124. If your child has a runny nose the first day of kindergarten, don't send the poor little kid to school. He will forever be known as Booger or Candles.

125. If your child has a gas problem, treat it medically. He could go through life being called Blurt, Stinker, Pong or Thunder Bum.

126. If your child is prone to throwing up in stressful situations, be prepared to call him Ruth, Ralph or Chuck Chunder for the rest of his life.

127. Parents, run through the rhyming name game before you slap down a name on a poor unsuspecting little child. You would be amazed at what horrid things rhyme with your child's name.

128. If teeth need fixing, go ahead and get them done early. It's hard to throw names like Bucky and Fang once they have been attached.

129. For those of you who are rhyming slang impaired: hemorrhoids are piles; piles rhymes with Farmer Giles.

130. If your name is Mark, that's close to Markus, which rhymes with Farcus, which when combined becomes Markus Farcus (a good name for any brother-in-law). Can you see how much fun this is?

131. The next time someone says, "What's in a name?" Punch him. He obviously never grew up in Australia.

132. Bravery and beliefs are not mutually exclusive.

133. Given a choice of fight or flight, Cliffy chose fight and flight. Unusual, but effective.

134. Be careful of the quiet ones; their reactions might surprise you.

135. After this Dad always said, "If you have to hit, there should only be two hits. You hitting him and him hitting the pavement."

136. This story made Dad a legend in his kids' minds.

137. The next time someone on the highway cuts you off and you want to react, just imagine waking up on a median strip with a very sore jaw, an aggravated wife, and lots of snarled traffic behind your car. You might just change your mind!

138. You can't judge a cubicle by its shoes.

139. Never assume that what you saw go into the toilet is what is actually sitting there.

140. The Farrell clan is apparently immune to large doses of Epsom Salts (Exlax).

141. Bowels and bladders must be infinitely expandable because Farrell didn't go to the bathroom for the remaining three days of camp.

142. Quick and effective random abstract thinking is hard to come by in stressful situations.

143. You should never attempt to give the camp director a swirly. He could turn out to be your father-in-law one day.

144. The "Vinny Barbarino" defense of "What? Where? And When?" doesn't work if your wife sees you toss the poor little pus-eyed kitten bag in the water.

145. If you break down under cross-examination, at least give some semblance of the truth as your explanation.

146. Newly married men are morons.

147. Cats still hate me. Especially poor little pus-eyed kittens.

148. If you ever see a poor little pus-eyed kitten, just turn and leave.

149. What is funny to a newly married man is often not funny to his newly married wife.

150. Men, learn to say, "Honey, you were right and I was wrong!" Practice it. It won't roll easily off that neophyte tongue at first, but it will come in handy sooner than you think.

151. If you accept money to take a life and dispose of the body, is that a bad thing?

152. If you keep your elbow in, head low, and use a discus spin you can get good distance with a bag of poor little pus-eyed kittens.

153. To this day, my wife fears getting conjunctivitis and finding a house brick and Hessian bag in the trunk of our car.

154. Guys, timing is everything. Never hire out for a hit while you are on your honeymoon.

155. Small things can have big consequences.

156. Little packages sometimes pack a big wallop.

157. Check with your neighbors before you run your animals through their yards.

158. Love me? Love my dogs.

159. Exactly how far is far enough away?

160. You can't write "Dogs Criticized" on the U.S. immigration card asking the reason why you left Australia.

161. You can criticize me, you can criticize my husband, but if you criticize my dogs, you're done for.

162. The simpler the task, the more difficult the concept appears to be.

163. You can always rely on a spider monkey to get the job done.

164. No one wants to be shown up by a spider monkey.

165. Sometimes the not-so-subtle hints work the best.

166. Wait a minute. If the monkey can handle the PC tapes, then the monkey can handle the mainframe tapes! I could be replaced?

167. Repetition does not make you learn unless you really want to learn.

168. It would never have really worked because the spider monkeys would have felt lonely when they didn't get to take a twenty minute smoke break every hour.

169. Vinyl siding melts when you hold an open flame to it.

170. Wood siding has a higher flame point than vinyl siding.

171. Any normal person would learn from early life experiences not to make flaming paper torches.

172. You can't swat flying wasps with a flaming newspaper.

173. In a wasp attack, given the choice of going for cover in a confined space or running up the street, always run up the street. You can always keep running.

174. The cost of wasp spray is always less than siding repair and medical bills.

175. We don't give blind people enough credit for what they have to put up with.

176. Bored adults are just as bad as bored five-year-olds.

177. There is always a scientific test for a reasonable question.

178. People will go to amazing lengths to find a safe and secure bathroom. Some would even drive home.

179. CEO's don't have a sense of humor.

180. I didn't learn from past experiences that shoes do not a person make.

181. We never did learn the answer to our question.

182. At least I didn't kick in the door and sing happy birthday to the guy.

183. Sometimes people don't even know when a joke has been played on them.

184. Be kind to your employees and they will be kind to you.

185. You should always try to carry a good 2-shilling handkerchief.

186. You should always keep some small denomination notes in your wallet. You might need them for more than tipping.

187. Bosses can start new office fashion trends. The sockless loafer look might just catch on.

188. If you suspect that people are taking you for granted, test it out.

189. It never hurts to plant a seed of doubt about what might be in the projects you're covering for other people. They tend to read things more closely after an incident like this.

190. If a twenty-five percent pay increase didn't stand out in the budget review, I was definitely not being paid enough.

191. Presidents don't have much of a sense of humor.

192. Take the time to check what other people do for you and thank them for their effort.

193. White men can jump.

194. NBA Scouts are never around when you need them.

195. Gravity can be defied when jumps are assisted by frantic arm waving movements.

196. Wafted wasp killer just annoys wasps.

197. I scream like a girl.

198. I hate yellow jackets.

199. I hate snakes.

200. Neighbors are often no help at all.

201. There is a direct relationship between the level of embarrassment of a situation and the number of people watching.

202. You can't explain to a laughing neighbor what happened when you have drool running from your mouth, you can't feel you face, and you can't "pronounth yo wodths."

203. No matter how old they are, boys and their toys will always get into trouble.

204. I now know how a fish feels when it is out of water.

205. Testosterone will overcome rational thinking every time.

206. Gravity bites.

207. Kids like to dial 911. In some homes they get a lot of practice.

208. Mowing the yard is a task, not a quest.

209. You have gone too far if you wear sunglasses, camouflage gear, attach loud speakers to the mower and play Sousa music to get the kids to run from you as you cut.

210. "Winning" may not be everything, but it's better than "embarrassing."

211. After this, every time I mowed the lawn my neighbors would yell, "Buckle up Bozo!" as they drove past.

212. The "Hey Y'all Watch This!" Hall of Fame has a place reserved just for me.

213. Sometimes you just need to spank a child as a reference point for change.

214. It's hard to gag and spank at the same time.

215. No matter how many times you flush, plastic tea cups just won't go down.

216. Just when you think things couldn't get any worse, they will.

217. It's hard to replace pink teacups so they match the rest of the set.

218. You get back what you gave early in life.

219. Does this mean my kids will always suffer from "potty mouth?"

220. Supervise, supervise, supervise. That's all I am going to say.

221. Apparently, it's not a real party until someone drinks from the toilet.

222. Kids can go from adorably cute to precociously embarrassing in 6.2 seconds.

223. People can apparently read upside down when in embarrassing situations.

224. Desk clerks will always fall back on the old "Oh, I have to get under my desk now to find something" routine, leaving everyone else to suffer.

225. Sometimes the truth hurts. I have two laser burns to prove it.

226. If you weigh more than one hundred pounds, just say NO to Spandex.

227. I now know what Dad meant when he said someone was "two axe handles across the rear end!"

228. I can never look at saddlebags without thinking of that special day.

229. I can take solace in the fact that one day it will be MY turn to embarrass my daughter.

230. The Daddy's prayer doesn't work, but I still thank God every day for my daughter.

231. If you are a cat, fear me and fear my children!

232.Cataclysm—a violent event marked by overwhelming upheaval and demolition.

233.Catatonic—a stupor marked by a lack of movement or activity.

234.Catastrophe—a momentous tragic event ranging from extreme misfortune to utter overthrow or ruin.

235.All these words start with "Cat," deal with disaster, and relate to my family. Coincidence? I think not!

236.Five-year-old Shepherd children have a tendency to pay too much attention to cats.

237.Just once in your life you mow eight cats, and people hold that against you for the rest of your life.

238.Hey! At least the litter was baptized!

239.Whenever I hear the word kitty litter, you can guess what flashes before my eyes.

240.Dogs don't know the difference between "A Cat" and "The cat." Cats are just cats.

241.This was my first use of the line "What were you thinking!" It would not be the last use, as history would show.

242.A cat will stay in a basket just like water will stay in a bucket as you spin it around.

243.You <u>can</u> scare the poop out of someone.

244.The speed of the spin is directly proportional to the pitch of a cat's howl.

245.Cats are mean and take pleasure in taunting dogs.

246.Dogs can be as dumb as a bag of hammers.

247.The real difference between "A Cat" and "The Cat" is the speed of the cat.

248. A father's reaction time is inversely proportional to the humor found in the situation before him. The funnier it is, the slower you react.

249. The pitch of the synchronized howl is determined by how hard you pull the cat.

250. Never assume that the high ground is the safest place to be.

251. You can shave a cat, but it won't like it.

252. Unlike poodles, you can't be stylishly creative when you shave a cat. Patterns are out and a bouffant look is impossible.

253. Cats hold grudges.

254. Cat Shaving as an Olympic event? I vote yes!

255. Someone should start cat shaving therapy sessions for frustrated cat owners.

256. There is only one thing scarier than waking up with a cat's bottom sitting on your face. That's right, waking up with a shaved cat's bottom sitting on your face.

257. The apple doesn't fall far from the tree.

258. Cats play with their food.

259. You can be really creative with your family activities.

260. It's not how high the score is in the game, it's who scores last that really counts.

261. Timing is everything in "Whack a Mouse."

262. Its all fun and games until the dead mouse lands on your head.

263. Always read the fine print.

264. Never trust a cabana boy.

265. For that matter, you should probably never trust your sister.

266. Never ask yourself how bad could this be, because it will always get worse.

267. I now know how frustrated a sperm whale can be.

268. The need for self-preservation will overcome brotherly love any day.

269. I will always be able to recognize an atomic bathing suit wedge from a distance.

270. The pounding of an open ocean Jet Ski ride does cure a bad case of hemorrhoids.

271. When it comes to the pucker factor, you can take it from 0 to 10 but you can never go back to 0.

272. I now know how my bait feels when I fish.

273. No matter how hard and how often you clench your bottom cheeks, they will not keep you on a surf ski.

274. Never, ever, ever leave your wife alone and hyped up on Cocoa on Christmas Eve.

275. Kids are smart and can recognize a cover-up when they see one.

276. Never, ever, ever, tell a child that there is no Santa. Deny, deny and deny again any question of his non-existence.

277. Hot tubs will never be the same for me again.

278. Timing is everything. Wait until your kids are married to set reality straight.

279. You can never underestimate the fearless energy of an excited ten-year-old girl.

280. Time certainly does change your perspective on what constitutes fun.

281. You can't get three hundred and fifty pounds of flour in a two hundred pound bag. (Well, you actually can, but it ain't pretty.)

282. Never let testosterone make decisions for you.

283. Oxygen is a good thing. Use it wisely and never sparingly.

284.Mass and acceleration can overcome inertia in the blink of an eye.

285.If you watch the kayak broadcast from the Olympic white water rafting circuit and you look really closely at rapid five you can actually see two shoe width plough marks leading down to the water's edge.

286.In a war of nerves a cat will always win.

287.Cover your garbage or put it out before going to bed.

288.It's amazing what a difference five minutes can make in your life.

289.Is there a cat CPR course that owners can take?

290.Fear the fractious cat!

291.Cats are patient.

292.Cats know where you sleep.

293.Cats rule the night.

294.Remember, you eventually have to go to sleep.

295.If you like your cat, you should never leave plastic food bags in your garbage.

296.Sometimes you regret letting the cat out of the bag.

297.There is only one thing worse than an annoying cat, and that's a "crazy annoying cat."

298.Never bite the hand that feeds you.

299.Cuddle Huddles are less snuggles and more trouble than they are worth.

300.Even in death, the cat can still stick it to a father.

301.Does the cost of future therapy for my children really offset the emotional cost of the cat's reign of terror?

302.Always keep some blue frog dart poison handy. You never know when you might need it.

303. Never close more than one door between you and a possible rescue squad.

304. Remove all decorative paraphernalia from a candle before using it under industrial conditions.

305. Never, I repeat, NEVER, assume that wadded paper will snuff out a burning ember.

306. Never put flaming objects between your bare legs.

307. Burning paper floats AND CONTINUES TO BURN.

308. In the time it takes for burning toilet tissue to make two rounds of a toilet bowl, it can do a lot of damage.

309. Gravity sucks.

310. You should never make fat people carry stuff.

311. The next time you eat a pear, I know what you will be thinking!

312. I am thinking about having snaps sewn to my waist and fitted to my underwear.

313. Fat people should always wear clean underwear and nice socks.

314. Long-tailed shirts also help in embarrassing situations.

315. Perhaps a naked fat person protest might encourage the fashion world to address our little problem.

316. The next time my pants drop to the floor, I'm stepping out and moving on without them.

317. The words "Walk," "Mountain," and "Chalet" should never be used in the same sentence and have been stricken from my personal vocabulary.

318. Anyone who will pay $85 per person to experience what I went through, "just ain't right."

319. Near death experiences tend to change your perspective on personal violence.

320. I need to do more weight lifting than just "getting out of bed" each morning.

321. The description "Romantic Night" is a misrepresentation when you and your spouse share a room with "Ted and Alice" in the bunk up above.

322. The next time my wife tells me we're going to a remote chalet for the night, there had better be a donkey, lama, motorcycle, car or helicopter involved in the transportation process.

323. People are stupid. At least some of them are. Well, maybe just one.

324. Proper prior planning prevents…ah, who am I kidding; nothing could have kept this guy out!

325. The apple doesn't fall far from the tree.

326. There is no relationship between "the quality of the camping experience" and "the amount of money spent to set that experience up."

327. State Parks should require deep background and personality checks on all future campsite registrations.

328. I must research if State Parks really mean "No firearms" and whether they had Bob and Son of Bob in mind when they made that decision.

329. Further, was this rule set up to protect the campers, or Bob and Son of Bob?

330. I will be adding cyanide pills to our camping equipment medical kit (to prevent death by boredom).

331. The tribal dance will never be dead.

332. Daddies hear gunslinger music in their heads when they look at boys wooing their daughters.

333. Dress codes change from generation to generation.

334. Rule number 1—No Touching!

335. Rule number 2—If he makes her cry, I make him cry!

336. If you must show me your underwear, just wear them on the outside of your pants.

337. Hats are not a fashion accessory, they are just hats. Traditionally, they do not serve any mating ritual function.

338. Men are pigs. I know, I used to be a man before I got married.

339. Daddies, in the thirteen-year-old gift game of cards, be the first to throw the wild card.

340. No matter how old she gets, she will always be my baby girl.

341. Fear puberty.

342. Sex education is an adult conspiracy to confuse the young.

343. We need to get sex off the front page of our minds and back into the deep recesses of mystery and folklore where it really belongs.

344. When you buy your next dictionary, black out the word "sex" and its definition with a felt tip marker. You could save an eight-year-old from a fate worse than death.

345. When you mother asks you if you learned anything in sex education just say "YES!"

346. Veiled innuendo and mysteries are often better than the truth.

347. Going to the toilet will not send you blind. However, there seems to be a correlation between getting older, spending longer in the toilet, developing hemorrhoids, and your eyesight gradually going bad.

348. The people next to you frown upon a "hands-off" contortionist act at the urinal.

349. You cannot get "the pox" from sleeping. What a relief that was after many sleepless nights!

350. The answer is "a Bed," not the room, house or street.

351. "The Pox"—apparently a colorful description of any generic social disease.

352. "Dibs and Dabs"—rhyming slang for "the crabs" or body lice.

353. You cannot tell the difference between a dib and a dab. Well, at least not without a very good microscope and the Eighth Edition of "Simon's Field Guide to Sexing Body Lice."

354. The secret tribal code of "Sex Education" can never really be fully broken. Let's keep it that way.

355. I could never eat carrots after that day without thinking of certain consequences.

356. When the tough questions get asked, fall back on folklore, innuendo and fear. It worked for me.

357. Someone doesn't have to say; "I love you" for you to know you're loved.

358. Change is okay.

359. You don't have to live up to everyone else's standard. Make your own and be comfortable with it.

360. Everyone should start a simple family tradition.

361. Whisker kisses are fun. Go ahead, enjoy!

362. Remember, you never know when you might be getting your last whisker kiss.

363. There are some things that you just can't explain.

364. You are never asked to bear more than you are able.

365. Christian friendships are timeless.

366. God will find a way.

367. Never underestimate the power of prayer.

368. Be careful what you pray for; you just might get it.

369. Dad had a sense of humor about everything, even death. I can see him, shoulders slumped, head bowed forward, laughing over the discomfort his size caused.

370. The strangest things in life can bind brothers and brothers-in-law together. Some memories are priceless.

371. Self-preservation and the fear of "great huge holes" sometimes override the need to show brotherly love.

372. Appearance (stately movement to the grave) and reality (not going to make it, not going to make it!) are two different things.

373. Go for the feet first, even if you have to knock people down.

374. Never send an eighteen-year-old girl and an eighty-year-old guy to do five people's work.

375. When we say "big" we mean "BIG."

376. There may be a future for tag team pall-bearing.

377. Take time to think about your children's future in terms other than success and riches.

378. Ask yourself if your loved ones really know how you feel about them.

379. The process of preparing the prayer will change your own priorities in life.

380. Draw on your own parent's unwritten hopes and expectations to help you navigate life's trials and tribulations.

381. Pray for your children every day.

382. Just say no to "snaking."

383. Always question if they wiped off the snake after their last colonoscopy.

384. When checking out a new doctor, ask what his handicap is before you decide on choosing him.

385. When you see an up-linked golf cart on a green with some guy working Edward Scissor Hand controls, don't sneak up and say boo! You could hurt someone.

386. We really do need to find more stuff for bored five-year-olds to do!

387. If you look hard enough, there can be a bright side to everything. Okay, sometimes you have to look "really, really hard."

388. In Mexico, if you don't have religion when you get into the cab, you will have it when you leave.

389. Your anatomy can learn to do new and wondrous things.

390. In Mexico, if you do get into a cab and it has more than three religious icons accompanied by a recorded message telling you to "Please hold on to the bar," back out quickly and leave.

391. In Mexico, if the driver throws back his head, laughs and screams, "Rules, we don't need no stinking rules!", you're definitely in trouble.

392. I have decided that we have been doing it all wrong in trying to convert people to our church. We are way too subtle. We must threaten converts with imminent physical death.

393. Our church should be training taxi drivers, not missionaries!

394. In our church taxi service, we would need a failed water jump attempt at the end to get people saved.

395. Some of the other churches might just need a drive-through car wash.

396. A certain Old Testament religion might only need to cut three inches off the exhaust pipe of the taxi at the end of each run.

397. No matter how benevolent the reign, the natives are always restless.

398. Even the king can be swayed.

399. The court jester should always mind his mother.

400. Kamikaze skunks? Perhaps a plot to take over our backyard?

401. Our dufus dogs don't know the difference between playing and killing.

402. Natural causes? Apparently any death other than by bullet wound.

403. Sometimes the simplest of things can say, "I love you and miss you."

404. A son needs a father as much as a father needs a son.

405. Sometimes a father has to do hard things to keep the family fed.

406. A son can step in for his father and fill his shoes when he is away.

407. You can face your fears and win.

408. Help your children develop, seek and follow their dreams.

409. Support your child's goals even if they are not exactly what you planned for them.

Boy, that is quite a list. I hope that you take my advice and put them all to good use. Oh, and don't forget to start your own list of important life lessons to remember!

Take Care,

Daddy
December 18, 2002

About the Author

Born in Sydney in 1956 to Cliff and Audrey Shepherd, Ian spent the first six years of his life living in Granville, a working class suburb of Sydney, with his parents and grandparents. These formative years were spent mostly under the tutelage of his grandmother who provided day care while the rest of the family worked hard to get their own home built. Some of the early stories of his life date to this period and give an interesting insight into the mind of an active young Aussie with time on his hands.

 In 1962 the family moved to their new home in Blacktown, a small outer rim suburb of Sydney that had just begun development. The author spent the next twenty-five years in this area completing high school and finalizing a degree in Marketing from the University of Western Sydney (Nepean). It was during these years that the importance of family and church were imprinted on his impressionable mind.

In 1979 Ian married a life long friend, Dee Ann Roper a missionary's daughter, and took up residence in Marayong, a suburb of Sydney. After living and working in the area for nine years they made plans to further their education in America. In 1987 Ian and Dee Ann moved to Nashville Tennessee where they both entered school, Ian to complete his M.B.A. and Dee Ann to complete her Bachelor of Science degree in Music Education. It was during this time that Tabitha (1988) and Ethan (1991) their children were born.

Ian spent many years working in industry in both Australia and the United States. In all his experience he was noted as having a unique sense of humor regarding the workplace and his home life. "After all," Ian would say, "If I can't laugh at the silly and stupid things I have done, my life would be pretty boring?" He is also known to tell a good story around the campfire.

After completing his M.B.A. Ian continued his education while working and in 1998 completed a Doctor of Arts degree in Economics from Middle Tennessee State University in Murfreesboro, Tennessee. In August of 2002, Ian moved to

Montgomery Alabama where he is now Chairman of the Department of Business at Faulkner University.

Ian calls himself a "humorist", trying to see the funny side of all the events that befall us in life. His stories and humor reflect on the everyday man and his ability to find joy in the simplest of things, mainly his own stupidity.

0-595-27880-9